A Lifetime of Stories

Andrew McKean

D1521716

Bundanoon, NSW, Australia.

November 2024

Table of Contents

A Lifetime of Stories

My Earliest Memory

I can still recall the warmth of the fire as I sat in the lounge room with my parents. The year was 1946, and though I was young, the moment stands out in my mind like a snapshot from a time gone by. My father, who worked at the Royal Melbourne Hospital, had invited a guest that afternoon, someone unlike any of our usual visitors. He was a soldier, an American, convalescing after the war, and it was the first time I had ever met anyone from the United States.

There was something captivating about him, though I could not have said why at the time. Perhaps it was the way he carried himself, as if the weight of the world rested on his shoulders, yet he wore it lightly. Or perhaps it was his accent, so different from anything I had heard before. He said he was from Wisconsin, a place that sounded distant and strange, almost otherworldly to my young ears. He spoke of his work as a fireman there, and though I could not fully grasp the meaning of his words, I was entranced by the rhythm of his speech, the unfamiliar cadences that made ordinary conversation seem like something out of a storybook.

I remember watching the flicker of the flames in the hearth, feeling the presence of something larger than myself—something tied to the world beyond our small home. That afternoon marked the first time I began to understand that the world was wider and more mysterious than I had ever imagined.

An Electronics Nerd

I've been interested in electronics for most of my life. It all started back in 1950 when I was ten years old. My father, always supportive of my curiosity, helped me build a crystal set. I can still remember the thrill of hearing that first faint crackle of a radio station. It felt like magic!

Soon after, I got my hands on some radio valves and built a shortwave radio. It required an external antenna, so we found an old flagpole and set it up in the backyard. At first, the neighbours were a bit worried, but when they realised I could tune into stations from around the world, they became just as fascinated as I was.

A turning point came when I discovered an amateur radio enthusiast living nearby. He and his wife kindly welcomed me into their home, where they had a proper "shack" full of equipment. I was in awe! They let me observe and learn, and soon enough, I was hooked on amateur radio.

A few years later, I had my own amateur radio station, complete with a beam antenna, which I operated on the 2-metre band. It was an incredible experience. Around this time, my father enrolled me at the Melbourne Technical College for a two-year, full-time course in electronics. This was in 1954, just as television was being introduced to Australia. By the time I was 16, I had qualified as an electronics technician – just as the world of television was starting to take off.

Looking back, those early experiences laid the foundation for a lifelong passion. Electronics has been a constant thread throughout my life, and it all started with a crystal set and a bit of curiosity.

The Gatekeeper

Bendigo Street, Richmond was a quiet street except at the hour when the Heinz soup factory set the workers free. The red brick factory of three storeys stood at number 22, detached from its neighbours in a large square ground. The other houses of the street, conscious of decent lives within them, gazed at one another with brown imperturbable faces.

The former tenant of the factory, a piano manufacturer, closed for business in 1935 and the building was sold that same year to the Heinz soup company. Musty from having been long enclosed, and littered with old useless vats and machines, the building was again sold in 1955, to a consortium of newspaper publishers, radio stations and theatre companies. A chimney stood in the centre of the factory grounds and for 50 years it belched smoke, soot and ash over the neighbourhood. Of no architectural significance its only appeal was that from the very top, and on a clear day, the recently built GTV transmitter tower could be seen atop Mount Dandenong 35Km to the East, providing a line-of-sight path for a microwave link.

Jago Street, which defined the northern boundary, led to a side entrance and the gatehouse where Bert had spent most of his working life as the gatekeeper, all the other

Heinz workers having long since gone. He witnessed the steady stream of celebrities, the toing and froing of the early days of television from 1956 onwards. Bert was everyone's friend, with a welcoming smile to help us start a long and tedious day. For some strange reason he took a liking to me and often invited me to visit his house nearby for lunch, where he lived with his wife Mary, on the pretext of adjusting his new TV set.

They lived in a modest weatherboard cottage, a short walk from the television station. The living room had that cozy lived-in feeling, yet there was an air of sadness amid the warmth and hospitality. A shiny new Astor SJ 17inch TV sat in one corner and a fireplace with a mantelpiece above, in another. Mary would prepare a nourishing meal of crumbed fish, mashed potatoes and vegetables. The table was set with her finest cutlery and crockery, and the meal was brought to the table where the three of us sat. They did not eat, but just sat there quietly watching me as I enjoyed the meal. Afterwards I would check-over their TV, adjust the fine-tuning, set the brightness and contrast and generally make a fuss over nothing, as the set was in perfect order.

On a subsequent visit I noticed that on the mantelpiece there was one solitary framed photograph, of a young man in military uniform, he would have been around my age at the time. Bert and Mary would always accompany me to their front gate and see me off on the short walk back to the studio, to the mayhem and chaos of the afternoon rehearsal for the Tarax Happy Show.

The Car Pool

It was 1959, and Graham Kennedy had just taken delivery of a brand-new white Holden FC station wagon. He'd traded in his beloved Vauxhall and was itching to show off the Holden on a jaunt to Geelong for an outside broadcast of IMT. The entire GTV9 crew was often deployed to various locations on Friday nights, and this trip had been in the works for ages. Being close to Melbourne, a car pool was organised, and the notice usually went up outside the maintenance department on Thursday.

The station buzzed with chatter and friendly jostling about who would score a ride with Graham, the station's most flamboyant and adored personality. Who would it be? There was room for at least two passengers. Surely it would be Panda and Tom Miller, the producer. The person preparing the list faced a real conundrum! In the end, they hit on the perfect solution: pair the most popular with the second most popular, and toss in the most introverted person on the staff for good measure.

On Thursday, the noticeboard was a hive of activity, with everyone peering and speculating. Finally, the list went up:

G. Kennedy, J. Allen, A. McKean

I barely slept that night. On the day of the

broadcast, I was waiting nervously in the GTV9 maintenance department. Graham strolled in with a broad smile, "Where's Andrew?" he called. I peeked out from behind a camera I was tinkering with and introduced myself. "Come with me," he said, and I followed him to the car park, acutely aware of the envious stares. There it was, his gleaming new FC Holden. To my astonishment, he walked to the passenger side, opened the door, and beckoned me to sit. Shortly after, Joff Allen arrived and took the rear seat. We set off, Graham driving with great care, as the car was brand new.

Navigating through Melbourne's bustling streets, we stopped at the traffic lights at Swanston and Bourke. "Look, isn't that Graham? And Joffa! Who's that young guy in the front?" The traffic stopped, pedestrians gawked and pointed. The lights turned green, and I couldn't resist giving a cheeky royal wave as we glided past. During the trip to Geelong, I sat in awe, listening to Graham and Joffa's non-stop stories and laughter. I hardly said a word.

Upon arriving in Geelong, Graham found the OB van and dropped me off with a courteous handshake and smile, as did Joffa. I scurried into the van, just in time for rehearsal.

Graham had impeccable manners and a unique ability to make people feel at ease. He was a true gentleman, admired and respected by all—a real top bloke, the nicest person I've ever met.

A Passage to England

In December 1961, at the age of 21 and very much single, I embarked on a grand adventure aboard the P&O liner Himalaya. The five-week voyage to London promised an array of exotic destinations, each stop a new chapter in our unfolding story. Alongside me were my three best mates: all of us fresh-faced, full of dreams, and ready to embrace the world beyond our familiar Australian shores.

We had all worked together at GTV9, a bustling television station in Melbourne. It was a place that had seen us grow from nervous novices to confident technicians, handling everything from cameras to cables. The friendship we forged in the control rooms and studios was now propelling us across the seas, seeking new experiences and opportunities in far-flung lands. Our first stop was Bali, a paradise of swaying palms and shimmering sands. We spent our days exploring the island, marvelling at its vibrant culture and the warmth of its people. Next came Singapore, a city of contrasts where sleek modernity met rich traditions. The hawker stalls, the bustling markets, and the impressive skyline left us in awe. Colombo offered a taste of the exotic East, with its colonial architecture and fragrant spice markets. We wandered through its streets, soaking in the vibrant atmosphere. Aden, on the other hand, was a stark contrast: a barren, rocky landscape that spoke of ancient trade routes and maritime lore.

As we passed through the Suez Canal, the engineering marvel of its time, we couldn't help but feel a sense of awe. The canal's significance was palpable, a gateway between worlds. Port Said greeted us with its bustling port and eclectic mix of cultures, a brief yet memorable interlude. Athens brought us face to face with history, the Acropolis standing as a testament to ancient civilisations. We wandered through its ruins, imagining the lives of those who once walked the same paths. Naples, with its chaotic charm and delicious cuisine, was a sensory delight. The scent of pizza and the sight of Mount Vesuvius made a lasting impression. Barcelona was a whirlwind of art and architecture, Gaudí's masterpieces leaving us spellbound. We spent our days exploring its streets, each corner revealing something new and wondrous.

Finally, we arrived at Tilbury Docks in London, our gateway to a new chapter. The journey was more than just a passage from one place to another. It was a voyage of discovery, of friendship, and of boundless possibilities. With the world at our feet and television stations in our sights, we were ready to take on whatever came our way.

Arrival in London

In early January 1962, at the age of 21, I arrived
at Tilbury Docks after a five-week voyage from
Melbourne, Australia. The journey had been
nothing short of wonderful, and I felt a pang of
sadness as I disembarked, leaving behind the
ship that had become a floating home.
Nonetheless, I was eager for the adventures that
lay ahead.

Along with my three travelling companions, I
boarded a train to London. Our destination was
Lancaster Gate, where we found a small hotel
that overlooked Hyde Park and the Serpentine.
It was the middle of winter, and the weather
was a stark contrast to what we had left behind
in Australia—cold, rainy, and shrouded in fog.
Despite this, our spirits were high, buoyed by
the promise of new experiences.

The first morning in London was a sensory overload. As we stepped out into the thick fog, I was immediately struck by the sights and sounds of this vibrant city. Mini-skirts, knee-high boots, long coats, and bowler hats mingled on the streets, while umbrellas bobbed up and down as people hurried along. Black cabs darted through the traffic, and red double-decker buses lumbered by, adding splashes of colour to the grey day. It felt like we had stepped into another world. The air buzzed with the energy of a city on the brink of cultural revolution. Mary Quant's bold fashion statements were everywhere, and the infectious beat of The Beatles was the soundtrack to our adventures. We danced the Twist at every opportunity, caught up in the fervour of the new dance craze that had taken the world by storm.

The city was also alive with scandal and intrigue. The Profumo affair was the talk of the town, and names like Christine Keeler were on everyone's lips. London was a place where anything seemed possible, and we were eager to soak it all in. Every moment was filled with discovery. From the foggy mornings in Hyde Park to the bustling evenings in Soho, London offered a feast for the senses. Though the winter chill bit through our coats, the excitement of being in this dynamic city kept us warm. It was the beginning of an adventure that would shape the rest of our lives, and I knew that these first impressions of London would stay with me forever.

After a few days we found a flat at Hillcrest Court, Shoot-Up Hill, on the corner of the A5 and Mill Lane, NW6, finally a place we could call home.

The Night Train to Glasgow

Mid-January 1962 in London was a pivotal moment in my career. Clutching a letter of introduction from my previous employer in Australia, I attended an interview at 9 Upper Berkeley Street, the London office of PYE TVT

Ltd. PYE, a Cambridge manufacturer of television studio equipment, had supplied much of the gear at the Melbourne television station where I had worked for five years. The interview was probably the easiest I had ever had; they were desperate for experienced engineers to install and support their products.

They wanted me to start immediately and solve an issue at Scottish Television, Glasgow. The problem was that they couldn't sync the video signal from their outside broadcast van with their studio, and the fault lay with a PYE Sync Slaving Unit. This device, known for its unreliability, required careful adjustment. Fortunately, I had two years' experience with the same equipment in Melbourne.

That evening, I found myself at Euston station, boarding the overnight train to Glasgow. I was booked into a sleeper cabin, which made for a fairly comfortable journey. Arriving the next morning, I went straight to the studios of Glasgow Television. The Chief Engineer was in a sorry state, clearly under pressure as his job depended on fixing this issue. However, the sight of a 21-year-old fresh off the boat from Australia was likely the last thing he wanted to see.

Within half an hour, I diagnosed the problem: a ten shilling electrolytic capacitor had failed, a common issue in those days. Replacing the faulty part restored the station to normal operation. Everyone in the control room breathed a collective sigh of relief. The Chief Engineer, immensely grateful, invited me back to his office and promptly offered me a job on the spot. I had to tactfully decline, explaining that I had just accepted my current position at PYE. In the "Swinging Sixties," having a technical skill made finding work in London remarkably easy.

This episode marked the beginning of an exciting chapter in my professional life, filled with new challenges and opportunities in the rapidly evolving world of television technology.

A Bold Departure

It was in November 1962 when I received the assignment that would take me to Brazzaville, deep in French Equatorial Africa. The country, a place I had known only from maps and newsreels, seemed a world away from the quiet order of my life in England. I was young, barely into my twenties, and though I had seen my fair share of work as a Television Studio Engineer for PYE TVT Ltd, nothing could have prepared me for what lay ahead.

At the time, PYE was making strides in expanding television technology into parts of the world where even electricity was sometimes unreliable. The "Cambridge Station," a relatively low-cost turnkey solution designed for developing countries, was our company's latest invention—a neat, compact setup that could be delivered, installed, and operational in a matter of weeks. It was meant to be an introduction, a toe dipped into the waters of modern broadcasting for nations that had, until now, been outside the global television network.

The assignment to install one of these stations in Brazzaville felt like both an opportunity and a test. I was to be sent alone—no team of fellow engineers, no familiar faces. At 22 years of age I would be the sole representative of PYE on the ground, responsible not only for the technical work but also for managing the logistics, liaising with local authorities, and ensuring the station went live on schedule.

I can still remember the conversation with my manager, a man as practical as they come, as he laid out the details of the job.

"It's a straightforward install," he said, with a calmness that belied the magnitude of the task. "But you'll be dealing with local officials, and there might be some... complications." He didn't elaborate on what those complications might be, but the look on his face suggested he knew something I didn't. In hindsight, I think he might have been aware of the political undercurrents in Africa at the time—the independence movements, the lingering colonial tensions—but that wasn't something discussed in detail at PYE. We were engineers, after all, not diplomats.

With little time to digest the enormity of the task, I threw myself into preparations. There were manuals to read, equipment lists to double-check, and countless forms to fill out before I could even think about stepping on the plane. The Cambridge Station, with its racks of monitors, cameras, and control units, would be shipped ahead of me. My job was to ensure that when it arrived, it would be installed correctly and functioning perfectly. I packed my own suitcase lightly—just a few shirts, a couple of books, and a notebook in which I would keep meticulous records of every stage of the installation. I wasn't sure how long I would be in Brazzaville, but I was prepared for anything.

The night before my departure, I sat alone in

my small flat, going over the plans one last time. It was an odd feeling, knowing that by this time tomorrow, I would be en route to a place I had never seen before, with no idea what to expect when I got there. There was a sense of adventure, of course—what young man wouldn't relish the chance to be sent on such an important mission? But there was also fear. Africa was an unknown quantity. I had read about the continent's rich history, its cultures, its struggles for independence, but none of that prepared me for the reality of setting foot in a country still finding its place in the post-colonial world. During the Nazi occupation of France during World War II, Brazzaville functioned as the symbolic capital of Free France between 1940 and 1943. The Brazzaville Conference of 1944 heralded a period of reform in French colonial policy. The French Congo "benefitted" from the postwar expansion of colonial administrative and infrastructure spending as a result of its central geographic location within French Equatorial Africa

(French: Afrique équatoriale française, or AEF) was a federation of French colonial territories in Equatorial Africa which consisted of Gabon, French Congo, Ubangi-Shari, and Chad. It existed from 1910 to 1958 and its administration was based in Brazzaville.. It had a local legislature after the adoption of the 1946 constitution that established the Fourth Republic. La Republique du Congo (Brazzaville), formerly the French Congo, which gained independence in 1960.

The flight from London was long, first to Paris to meet with the PYE agent there, for a briefing. The next day I boarded a magnificent Douglas DC8 with stops in places I had only heard of in passing—Marseille, Gabon, before finally landing in Brazzaville.

As I sat on the plane bound for Brazzaville, my mind drifted back to my childhood in Melbourne. I must have been no more than twelve when I first became fascinated by the dial on our neighbour's large radiogram. It was a magnificent piece of equipment, a hulking presence that dominated the lounge room, standing there like an altar to the mysteries of the wider world. The dial itself was a source of endless fascination for me, a window into distant lands I could only dream of. It was engraved with the names of shortwave stations from across the globe—places that, at that age, seemed impossibly exotic.

There were names like London, Cairo, and Moscow, all etched in neat script around the edge of the dial. But one name always caught my eye, one that seemed to stir something deep within me every time I saw it: Brazzaville. It wasn't a name I had ever heard spoken aloud, but it lingered in my imagination like a distant echo from a place beyond reach. I had no idea what kind of city Brazzaville was, or even where it was, but the name held a strange allure. It suggested a place far removed from the familiar streets of Melbourne, a place on the edge of the world where something important was happening—though what that might be, I couldn't begin to guess.

More than once, I found myself standing alone in front of that radiogram, trying to tune in to Radio Brazzaville. I would twist the heavy knob slowly, carefully, listening for the crackle of voices or music from that far-off city. But no matter how hard I tried, there was only static. A faint hiss, rising and falling like the waves of a distant sea, but nothing more. Brazzaville, it seemed, would remain a mystery, a name engraved on a dial, unreachable and unknowable.

Now, as I sat there on the plane, staring out over the vast African landscape below, it struck me how strange life can be. All those years ago, I had stood in that dimly lit room, hoping to hear the sounds of Brazzaville through the static, and now here I was, on my way to that very city. Perhaps I would even get the chance to visit the radio station in person, to stand where those voices should have come from all those years ago. It seemed a fitting end to the mystery, a circle closing after all these years.

I remember the oppressive heat hitting me like a wave as I stepped off the plane. The air was thick with humidity, the kind that clings to your skin and makes every breath feel heavy. I stood there for a moment, blinking in the bright sun, trying to take it all in. The airport itself was a small, dusty affair—nothing like the bustling hubs of Europe. I was greeted by a local representative, a man from the government who had been tasked with overseeing the television station's installation on their end. His name was Jean-Claude, and though his English was halting and my French was practically non-existent, we managed to communicate through a mixture of hand gestures and technical jargon.

The ride into the city was an experience in itself. Brazzaville was nothing like the Europe I knew. The streets were alive with people—women carrying baskets on their heads, children darting in and out of traffic, men lounging in the shade, watching the world go by. The buildings were a strange mix of colonial grandeur and modern decay. Whitewashed facades, peeling paint, and crumbling balconies spoke of a time when this city had been the jewel of French Equatorial Africa. Now, it was a place in transition, still grappling with its colonial past while trying to forge a new identity.

As we drove through the streets, Jean-Claude pointed out various landmarks—the government buildings, the market, the river Congo that separated Brazzaville from Léopoldville across the water. I nodded politely, though in truth, I was too overwhelmed to take it all in. My mind kept drifting back to the task at hand—the station, the equipment, the installation. What if something went wrong? What if the equipment didn't arrive on time, or worse, arrived damaged? These were the thoughts that kept me awake that first night in Brazzaville, lying on a thin mattress in a small hotel room that overlooked the bustling market square.

I couldn't help but feel the weight of the responsibility I had been given. I was here, alone, in a country I didn't know, tasked with bringing the future to a place that still seemed anchored in the past. Yet, there was something exhilarating about it all. This was my chance to prove myself, to show that I could handle whatever challenges came my way. Little did I know just how many of those challenges I would face in the weeks ahead.

First Days in Brazzaville

The morning after my arrival in Brazzaville, I woke to the persistent sound of street vendors setting up for the day below my hotel window. The heat had already settled in, thick and cloying, even at that early hour. Despite a restless night, filled with the dissonant hum of the market and my own thoughts racing, I felt a renewed sense of purpose. The Cambridge television station, the heart of my assignment, was scheduled to arrive today by air. I had little time to dwell on the uncertainties; today was about action.

At precisely eight o'clock, Jean-Claude arrived at my hotel. He was punctual, as always, his reserved manner tempered by a slight smile as we exchanged brief pleasantries. His French-accented English was formal, and my knowledge of his language was still in its infancy. Yet, as we got into his car, there was a growing sense of mutual understanding. We both knew today was pivotal.

The drive to the airport was much like my first journey into the city—dust rising from the road, pedestrians moving in a slow, steady rhythm under the morning sun. I caught glimpses of the Congo River in the distance, a looming presence that seemed to define the city as much as any building or street.

The airport, though small and unassuming, bustled with the anticipation of the day's arrivals. As Jean-Claude and I stood by the tarmac, we awaited the appearance of the Bristol Freighter that was carrying the precious cargo. This plane was no ordinary aircraft. It had somehow navigated an exhausting and complex flight from the UK, traversing thousands of miles to bring a fully operational television station to a country on the verge of broadcasting its first signals.

The Bristol Freighter was a rugged, capacious beast, built for both civil and military use. Its broad nose gave it a utilitarian look, while the wings, heavy and sturdy, seemed designed to endure whatever misfortunes the skies might offer. As it descended, I could feel the weight of my responsibility intensify. This wasn't just another job; this was history in the making.

When the Bristol Freighter finally landed and taxied to a halt, the ground crew immediately sprang into action. I stood to the side with Jean-Claude, watching as the wide front doors were opened to reveal the large wooden crates, meticulously packed and stacked with the components of the Cambridge station. The crates were an imposing sight, squeezed tightly into the Freighter's cavernous hold. I felt a surge of relief knowing the station had made it here in one piece—or so I hoped.

We watched as the crates were slowly unloaded, each one requiring careful handling to ensure no damage occurred. The sun beat down relentlessly, and I wiped the sweat from my brow, feeling the weight of the moment. Soon, these crates would hold the key to the first television station in this part of the world—a thought that both excited and terrified me.

The crates were loaded onto trucks that had been arranged by the local government, and Jean-Claude made sure everything was accounted for with a quiet efficiency. He was a man of few words, but I had come to appreciate his calm presence. I sensed he had seen many ambitious projects come and go in Brazzaville and that he carried a healthy skepticism for each one.

Before heading to the building that would house the station, Jean-Claude suggested we stop for lunch. He spoke of a French restaurant housed in one of Brazzaville's few luxury hotels, perched just above the mighty River Congo. I readily agreed, my stomach growling after a morning of tension and excitement.

The hotel was a striking contrast to the bustling streets outside. Inside, it was all polished marble, high ceilings, and the low murmur of well-heeled guests enjoying the cool respite from the heat. The restaurant itself had an expansive terrace that offered an unobstructed view of the Congo River as it rolled past, its surface catching the midday light in ripples of gold and silver.

The Congo river was enormous, broad and powerful, a force of nature that seemed to dwarf everything around it. It was five miles wide and the skyline of Leopoldville, the capital of the Belgian Congo could be seen in the distance on the other side of the river. The city was named Léopoldville by Henry Morton Stanley in honour of Leopold II of Belgium.

During the 1940s and 1950s, the Congo experienced an unprecedented level of urbanisation and the colonial administration began various development programmes aimed at making the territory into a "model colony". One of the results of the measures was the development of a new middle class of Europeanised African "évolués" in the cities. By the 1950s, the Congo had a wage labour force twice as large as that in any other African colony. The Congo's rich natural resources, including uranium—much of the uranium used by the U.S. nuclear programme during World War II was Congolese—led to substantial interest in the region from both the Soviet Union and the United States as the Cold War developed. As I gazed across I was oblivious to the turmoil and political upheavals that were taking place in the Belgian Congo, a pre-cursor to events that would soon engulf French Equatorial Africa.

We sat at a table near the edge of the terrace, the sound of the river a constant, comforting backdrop. Jean-Claude ordered for us—a series of dishes that, I soon learned, would be the first of many magnificent meals I'd enjoy here. The French influence on the cuisine was unmistakable: rich, fragrant sauces, perfectly roasted meats, and fresh bread that tasted like it had been baked just moments before. For a moment, as I sipped a cold glass of white wine and watched the river roll by, I forgot about the crates waiting back at the airport. This was a rare luxury, and I allowed myself to savour it.

The conversation with Jean-Claude over lunch was light, a mix of pleasantries and cautious talk of the work ahead. He was curious about the television station, about how it would change Brazzaville. I could sense his guarded optimism —after all, he had seen projects come and go, promises made and broken. But there was something in his eyes that suggested hope. Television, for all its modern trappings, represented progress. It was a window into the world beyond Brazzaville, a connection to something greater.

After lunch, we returned to the trucks, which had been patiently waiting. The heat of the afternoon was even more oppressive than earlier, but there was no time to linger in the comfort of the restaurant. The trucks rumbled down the uneven roads toward the building that had been prepared to serve as the television station. As we drove, I looked out the window at the streets and wondered how long it would be before these same people—these shopkeepers, market vendors, children playing by the roadside—would be watching the first images broadcast from the station I was here to install.

The building itself was modest but functional. It had been chosen for its central location and its ability to accommodate the necessary equipment. The walls, thick and sturdy, would protect the delicate electronics from the elements, and the space inside was large enough to house the studios and control rooms, and a transmitter. As we arrived, a small crowd had already gathered to watch the arrival of the crates. For many of them, I imagined, this would be their first glimpse of television equipment, their first encounter with a technology that, until now, had been distant and abstract.

I stood there for a moment, taking in the scene. The building, the crates, the people—all of it felt surreal, as if I were standing on the edge of something monumental. In many ways, I was. This was the beginning of something that would change lives, and I had the strange, humbling privilege of being the one to make it happen.

The Cambridge Station Unboxed

When we arrived at the building that had been designated to house the new television station, it was far from the pristine, organised workspace I had envisioned. The concrete floor, freshly poured and still rough in places, was covered in dust and debris. Channels for the laying of cables had been cut into the floor, but they were untidy, filled with remnants of the construction process. I surveyed the room with a sinking feeling. Television equipment is delicate, and the last thing I wanted was to introduce it into an environment where dust and disorder could cause issues later down the line.

I turned to Jean-Claude, who had accompanied me from the airport, hoping he might offer some assistance in finding a cleaning crew. He merely shrugged, the universal gesture of indifference. Tidiness, it seemed, was not a priority here. For a brief moment, I felt a surge of frustration. I had traveled thousands of miles to be here, alone and under pressure to get everything operational in a tight timeframe, and now I would have to start by cleaning the place myself.

With no one else stepping up to help, I grabbed a broom I found leaning against a wall and set to work. The room echoed with the sound of bristles scraping across the concrete as I pushed dust and debris into uneven piles. It was tedious work, but necessary. I needed a clean, organised space before I could even think about unpacking the equipment. As I swept, I hoped that someone might take pity on me and offer to lend a hand. But no one came. The handful of locals who had gathered to observe the unloading of the crates seemed content to watch me toil away without much concern for the state of the floor.

After what felt like hours of sweeping and dusting, I finally got the room into a state I could live with. It wasn't perfect—far from it—but it was clean enough to start bringing in the equipment without worrying about dust clogging delicate circuits or interfering with the cameras. By this time, the crates had been unloaded from the trucks and were sitting in a haphazard row outside the building, their wooden sides splintered from the journey and the rough handling during unloading.

We cracked open the first of the crates, revealing the equipment packed inside with precision and care. I breathed a small sigh of relief; everything appeared to be in good condition, no obvious damage from the long journey. With a group of local workers now on hand, we began lifting the pieces inside. The main item, the large control desk, was the centerpiece of the operation. This was where all the electronic switching systems, monitors, and controls for the broadcast would be housed, the nerve center of the entire station. It was heavy, a solid piece of engineering designed to withstand years of use, and it took several of us to manoeuvre it into place.

Once the control desk was settled into its corner of the room, we moved on to the other crates. The two cameras were next. They were much lighter but no less valuable, and I made sure they were handled with care. For the time being, I placed them carefully on the floor, still in their protective packing. I would install them later, once the control systems were fully operational.

In an adjoining room, I could hear the sounds of another installation happening simultaneously. A French-speaking engineer had arrived from Paris the day before to oversee the setup of the transmitter. The transmitter, as it turned out, was a Marconi model—manufactured in England, just like the PYE equipment I was responsible for. This fact, though initially only a curiosity to me, would soon become a source of unexpected tension.

The Marconi transmitter and the PYE Cambridge Station had both been ordered as part of the same project, and it seemed a logical enough pairing to me. Both were well-regarded names in British engineering, and both had put in the lowest bids when the government contracts were issued. But as I soon discovered, the choice of British-made equipment had not gone unnoticed by the French contingent, who were soon to arrive from Paris to operate the station.

Word began to spread among the local crew that the French television operators were less than pleased with the arrangement. Clearly, when the contracts had been put out to tender, it was expected that French companies would win the bids. After all, this was still French Equatorial Africa in many ways, even as independence crept closer. It would have made sense for French manufacturers to supply the equipment, and yet here we were, with British names stamped on every piece of gear in the building.

By the time I had finished overseeing the unloading and unpacking, the first murmurs of consternation had reached me. There was a growing unease among the French-speaking engineers and technicians about the predominance of British technology in what they considered to be their domain. It was an unspoken but palpable tension—nothing overt, but enough to make me aware that the choice of equipment might lead to more challenges down the road.

Despite the unease, the installation process continued. I focused on my task, ignoring the undercurrents of dissatisfaction as best I could. The control desk was in place, and I began the slow, methodical process of wiring everything together. Cables had to be run from the cameras to the control room, switches installed, monitors mounted in their frames. It was painstaking work, but it was work I knew well. Each wire, each connection brought me closer to my goal: the moment when Brazzaville would broadcast its first television signal.

In the meantime, the French engineer worked steadily on the Marconi transmitter in the next room. We nodded to each other in passing but exchanged few words. Our common language, in this case, was the technical work we both understood. Still, I couldn't help but feel a slight tension building between us, a sense that we were two representatives of different worlds —two countries, two histories, two ways of doing things. How this would play out when the French crew finally arrived, I could only guess.

For now, though, my priority was clear. I had a television station to build, and it would take all my focus and skill to get it done. I pushed aside the concerns about the French operators, about the equipment choices, and even about the less-than-ideal work environment. The task in front of me was what mattered, and if that meant grabbing a broom again tomorrow, so be it.

A Night at the Dance Hall

One evening, as I was caught up in the usual tangle of wires and control units at the station, Jean-Claude approached me with a suggestion. He thought I should take a break from the relentless pace of the studio installation and, as he put it, "meet the locals." He had been watching me work tirelessly for days, and I suspected he thought a change of scenery might do me some good. I was surprised, however, when he mentioned his plans: he was inviting me to a local dance hall that Saturday night. He said it was a rare thing, indeed, for a foreigner to be invited to such a gathering—especially a white foreigner like myself. I agreed, intrigued and, admittedly, a bit uncertain about what to expect.

The night of the dance, we left Brazzaville's relatively well-lit streets behind, plunging into the darkness of the surrounding countryside. I had grown accustomed to the city's nocturnal quiet, with its occasional glow of street lamps casting halos on dusty streets, but now we were driving into an all-encompassing blackness. It was an awe-inspiring sight; the stars shone brightly above, unobscured by any hint of city light, stretching endlessly across the African sky like a vast map of distant worlds.

After a drive that seemed to carry us deeper and deeper into the unknown, we finally arrived at a modest building. I suspected it was a church hall, though it could have been anything. Outside, the muffled thump of drums and the buzz of conversation spilled into the night air, punctuated by occasional bursts of laughter. Jean-Claude led the way, guiding me into the heart of the gathering. As we entered, I quickly realised that he and I were the only foreigners there, a fact that drew curious glances but was met with an overwhelming warmth.

The hall was packed to the brim with people, young and old, all moving to the music with an infectious energy that I could feel even from the doorway. Musicians crowded onto a makeshift stage at the far end of the room, playing instruments I could barely recognise, though their enthusiasm was unmistakable. The drums pounded a beat that seemed to fill the very air, a rhythm as intense and relentless as the equatorial heat outside. The musicians worked together in a frenzied unity, each beat flowing seamlessly into the next. It was mesmerising, unlike any music I had ever heard.

The dancers, too, were something to behold. They moved in unison, but not with the measured steps of the dance halls back home in London. Here, the dancing was loose, wild, and uninhibited, as if the music itself were moving through each person, dictating their steps and gestures. I watched, entranced, as couples spun and swayed, their bodies in perfect rhythm with the drums, the music building into a fever pitch, then breaking into a slow, languid melody before rising once more.

I couldn't help but feel a sense of distance, almost alienation, watching these dances unfold. London, where The Beatles had just signed their first recording contract, and the Twist and Chubby Checker were sweeping the dance halls, seemed an entire world away. The music, the movement, and the energy in that room were completely foreign to me—unlike anything I'd ever seen or heard. Yet, as unfamiliar as it was, there was something undeniably captivating about it, something that seemed to speak to a deeper part of myself, beyond culture or language.

As the evening wore on, Jean-Claude introduced me to several of the locals, most of whom were delighted to meet someone from so far away. They asked me about life in England, about the work we were doing at the station, and about the music back home. I tried to describe the Twist, the way it had taken London by storm, but it sounded oddly flat in the context of the wild energy surrounding me. Here, dancing was not a trend or a passing craze —it was a part of life, a shared language that needed no explanation.

At one point, Jean-Claude even nudged me toward the dance floor, a mischievous grin on his face. Hesitantly, I joined in, attempting to mimic the movements I saw around me. My efforts, I'm sure, were less than impressive, and I may have looked like a fish out of water amidst the fluidity of the other dancers. Yet, no one seemed to mind. They simply laughed, cheering me on as I fumbled my way through the steps, their laughter warm and genuine. For a brief moment, I felt myself let go, caught up in the music, the motion, and the friendship of the evening.

The night wore on, the music rising and falling like the breath of the crowd, the air thick with sweat and the scent of dust and earth. I lost track of time, mesmerised by the endless, pulsing energy of the dance hall. It was an experience I could never have imagined back in London, a world apart from the polished halls and neatly arranged dance floors I was used to. Here, there were no rules, no scripts—just the music, the dance, and a sense of shared joy that filled every corner of the room.

As we finally made our way back to the city in the early hours of the morning, I sat quietly in the car, my mind filled with the sights and sounds of the evening. The darkness pressed in around us, and the stars glimmered overhead, vast and infinite. I couldn't help but feel a deep sense of gratitude for the experience, for the chance to witness something so different and, in its own way, profoundly beautiful.

Jean-Claude glanced over at me, a knowing smile on his face. "Well," he said, "now you've seen the real Brazzaville."

And he was right. In that crowded, pulsing dance hall, surrounded by music and laughter, I had glimpsed a side of Brazzaville that went far beyond the walls of the television studio or the city's colonial architecture. It was a place of warmth, of vitality, of a spirit that no broadcast signal or camera lens could ever fully capture. And as we drove on, leaving the countryside behind and heading back into the city, I knew that this was a night I would carry with me long after I returned home.

The First Test Transmission

A few days had passed, and I was beginning to feel cautiously optimistic. The studio was far from the polished, high-tech environments I had worked in before, but it was finally starting to take shape. The control desk was fully wired, the cameras were operational, and I had most of the system connected and ready for the initial switch-on.

The cameras functioned perfectly. These were beautiful pieces of engineering, with a clarity that impressed even me, despite the dust that still lingered in the air. I spent most of one afternoon fine-tuning them, adjusting the lenses and testing different lighting setups to make sure they were ready for the station's first test transmission. The picture quality from the cameras was excellent—a clean, sharp feed that showed the progress we were making. Now, all that was left was to connect the studio video feed to the Marconi transmitter in the adjoining room and see if we could get a signal out to the airwaves.

With the final cable connection in place, I stepped back, eager to see the fruits of our labor. Jean-Claude stood nearby, watching silently, and I could feel the weight of his expectations. As I flipped the switch to send the video feed to the transmitter, I prayed that everything would work seamlessly.

But almost immediately, I could tell something

was wrong. The picture on the off-air monitor, which should have been a sharp and stable image, was distorted—filled with strange artefacts and smears of shadow. The contrast all wrong. It looked as though someone had taken a perfectly good signal and run it through a meat grinder. My heart sank. I stared at the screen, and then at the Marconi transmitter, and I knew the issue wasn't on my end. The cameras and control systems were functioning perfectly. The problem was clearly inside the transmitter. I turned to the French engineer who had been responsible for the Marconi installation. He was already frowning at the equipment, his brow furrowed in concentration. For a moment, I stepped back, hoping that he would quickly recognise the issue and resolve it. After all, this was his domain, not mine.

But the hours wore on, and the French engineer's frown deepened. He ran tests, peered at circuit diagrams, and scratched his head, but nothing seemed to fix the problem. Jean-Claude and I exchanged glances, but there was little I could do. This wasn't my equipment, and I didn't want to overstep. However, as the day dragged on and the engineer's frustration grew, I began to recognise something familiar in the fault. From my vantage point, I could see the characteristic distortion of a specific problem I had encountered years ago, back when I worked at a television station in Australia. The faulty image looked just like the result of a malfunctioning vacuum tube, or as we called them in England, a valve—a specific one that clamped the black level of the video signal to a stable reference point.

The French engineer was pacing now, clearly in a state of panic. The pressure to get the station operational was immense, and he was running out of ideas. It was a delicate situation; stepping in without being asked could cause a rift, especially given the tension that already existed between the British and French contingents over the equipment choices. But I also knew I had the solution.

With a deep breath, I decided to approach him. Using considerable tact and diplomacy—along with plenty of gestures and pointing at the relevant sections of the circuit diagram—I suggested the possible cause of the issue. I indicated the valve that I believed was responsible, using the word "valve" in English, hoping he'd make the connection to the French word "lampe." To his credit, the engineer, despite his frustration, listened intently. His eyes followed my finger on the diagram, and he seemed to grasp what I was trying to convey.

With a mix of uncertainty and a bit of hope, he checked the valve. Sure enough, it was faulty. He swiftly replaced the part, his hands moving with the speed of someone who had finally seen the light at the end of a long, dark tunnel. The replacement was quick, and as soon as the new valve was in place, we tested the signal again.

The moment the video feed reappeared on the monitor, it was as though a weight had lifted from the room. The picture was perfect—clean, crisp, and stable. The relief was palpable, not just from the French engineer but from everyone in the room. I allowed myself a quiet moment of satisfaction. It was a small victory, but in the context of this project, it felt enormous.

The French engineer, his panic now replaced by gratitude, turned to me with a wide smile. Although we didn't share a common language, the relief in his eyes and his appreciative nod said more than words ever could. From that moment on, we forged an unlikely friendship, despite the barriers of language and the lingering tensions between our countries. He acknowledged my experience and expertise, and I respected his willingness to listen and act when it counted.

Later that evening, in a rare moment of relaxation, the French engineer insisted on taking me out for a drink. We found ourselves at the same luxury hotel by the river, where the air was cooler, and the atmosphere was relaxed.

Over a bottle of fine French wine, we toasted the success of the day. Though our conversation was limited to the odd word and gesture, it didn't matter. The bond forged over a shared technical problem and its resolution was enough.

I leaned back in my chair, feeling the tension of the day slowly drain away. The River Congo flowed in the distance, dark and mysterious in the twilight, and for the first time since I had arrived in Brazzaville, I allowed myself to feel a sense of calm. The station wasn't operational yet, and there were still plenty of challenges ahead, but for tonight, we had achieved something important.

Tomorrow, the real work would begin again.

The French Production Crew

The next morning, the French production crew arrived at the television station, their arrival marked by the deep rumble of vehicles pulling up outside and the sharp clatter of voices. I had been expecting them, of course. Jean-Claude had mentioned that they were due to arrive that day, but nothing could quite prepare me for the look of stunned disbelief that crossed their faces as they stepped through the doors and took in their new workspace.

From the moment they laid eyes on me, I could tell something was amiss. They had clearly expected someone else—perhaps a polished, multi-lingual engineer from the heart of Cambridge, one of the top minds from the PYE factory in England. What they got instead was me—a young man from Australia, of all places, with a slightly rough-around-the-edges look and an accent they likely found as bewildering as everything else they were about to encounter.

I stood there in my work clothes, hands dusty from the previous night's efforts, offering a polite nod as they entered. Their shock was palpable. I could see it in their eyes as they took me in, their silent appraisal only broken by the murmured exchange of a few words in rapid

French. Their collective expressions seemed to ask the same question: This is the man who built the station?

It didn't take long for them to confirm their suspicions. They glanced around the room, eyes widening at the sight of the equipment and control panels. Everything was labelled in English—every switch, every dial, every piece of equipment bore the marks of a British company. There was nothing familiar to them, nothing resembling the equipment they had worked with in Paris, where the studio floors were paved with decades of refined French television production techniques.

To make matters worse, my grasp of the French language was as basic as could be. Sure, I could get by with a few key phrases—enough to order a coffee or ask for directions—but comprehending the finer details of a French restaurant menu or engaging in a technical discussion? That was well beyond my abilities. The previous night's dinner with the French engineer had been a delightful experience, but I had barely managed to decipher what I was eating, relying on guesswork and context rather than any deep understanding of the language.

The crew, all of them seasoned professionals from various television networks in Paris, were visibly disoriented. I could sense their discomfort as they moved around the control room, inspecting the equipment. Their expectations had been utterly upended. This was not the slick, high-end installation they had been prepared for. This was an English setup, built by a young Australian, and now they were tasked with making sense of it.

They gathered in a small huddle, talking in hushed tones, and I stood back for a moment, unsure of how to proceed. This was their domain now—production, live broadcasting. I had done my part by installing the equipment and making sure everything worked, but the task of operating the station would fall squarely on their shoulders. Yet, I could tell that they were hesitant to trust what they were seeing.

After a few minutes, one of the men, clearly the senior producer, stepped forward. He was tall and thin, with a stern face framed by silver hair. He wore an air of quiet authority, the kind of confidence that comes from years spent directing live television in Parisian studios. He addressed me in French, and though I caught only a few words, I understood the gist of what he was saying. He wanted to know how everything worked.

I swallowed hard, trying to summon the right words. There were some things that didn't require language, I reminded myself. I gestured toward the control desk, motioning for him to come closer. As he approached, I pointed at the main controls—the switches, the faders, the video feeds. I spoke in simple English, keeping my explanations to the basics, and used as much non-verbal communication as I could manage. Diagrams, hand gestures, and a lot of pointing.

The French crew gathered around, their initial

wariness giving way to cautious curiosity. As I moved through the system, demonstrating how to switch between camera feeds, adjust audio levels, and monitor output, I could see them slowly starting to make sense of it all. The equipment may have been unfamiliar, but they were professionals, and professionals know how to adapt.

Still, there was no getting around the fact that this was not what they had expected. The looks they exchanged with one another said it all. They had arrived in Brazzaville expecting a seamless transition from their Parisian studios to this new station, but instead, they were faced with an entirely different system. And, as I well knew, the British penchant for labelling everything in English only added to their frustrations.

There was a moment of awkwardness as they began to experiment with the controls, their fingers hesitating over the switches and dials. I stayed close, offering what help I could, pointing out the key functions they would need to familiarise themselves with. The senior producer, to his credit, began to settle into the role of leader. He directed his team with quiet commands, and gradually, they started to test the equipment in earnest.

Jean-Claude, who had been hovering in the background, watched the whole scene unfold with a quiet amusement. I caught his eye at one point, and he gave me a small, knowing smile. He, too, had probably expected this to be a smoother process, but he also understood that this was Africa, where nothing ever seemed to go as planned.

By the end of the morning, the French crew had gained some confidence with the controls. The senior producer, now more at ease, approached me with a nod of approval. Though we still struggled to communicate with words, the unspoken understanding between engineers had bridged the gap.

It was clear to me, however, that the challenges

ahead weren't just technical. The French crew had arrived expecting to bring a piece of Paris with them, but they were in a different world now, and this station would require a different approach. And while I might not have been the university-educated, multi-lingual engineer they had hoped for, I was the one who had built the station from the ground up—and that, I hoped, would eventually earn their respect.

As the day wore on, I found myself wondering how long it would take for us to truly work together as a team. But for now, at least, we had taken the first step. The equipment worked, and the crew was starting to understand it. The rest, as they say, would come with time.

The Reluctant Crew

In the days following their arrival, it became increasingly clear that the French production crew wasn't in any great hurry to get the station fully operational. There were two women and two men, as I recall, all of them seasoned professionals, but none seemed eager to dive into the work of planning broadcasts. Instead, they spent their time conversing quietly in French, sometimes animatedly, sometimes in subdued tones, but always in a language I could barely follow.

It wasn't lost on me that they almost certainly spoke English. A few of them had addressed me directly in English on occasion, especially when the technical details of the equipment demanded it. But when it came to the real discussions—the talks about scheduling, programming, and what would actually go on air—they reverted to French, leaving me standing on the outside of the conversation, straining to pick up fragments of meaning from the occasional word I recognised. It was frustrating, to say the least. This was supposed to be a collaborative effort, and yet they seemed content to exclude me from their discussions, whether intentionally or not.

Worse yet, it became clear they hadn't brought

much in the way of broadcast material with them. I had assumed they would arrive with reels upon reels of film from their Paris studios —movies, documentaries, and other pre-recorded content that could fill the station's early schedules while they got the live production side of things up and running. But, as the days passed, it became painfully evident that they had brought almost nothing with them.

I remember asking one of the crew members about it—a serious-looking woman who seemed to be in charge of the station's content planning. She gave me a vague smile and a dismissive shrug, as if to say, What can you do?

Finally, one morning, I got my answer. A small group of African government officials arrived at the station, their presence immediately commanding attention. They didn't say much, but they were accompanied by a large, carefully wrapped package that they carried with an air of solemnity, like it was some precious artefact. I watched as they brought the package into the control room and, after some careful handling, unwrapped it to reveal a single 16mm reel of film.

This, it turned out, was the sole piece of broadcast material they had brought with them —this one reel of film, entrusted to them by the local government. I couldn't hide my surprise. A station without content was like a ship without sails. What were they planning to broadcast? Had they not thought this through?

I watched as the reel was placed delicately on the control room table, the government officials exchanging quiet words with the French production crew, who nodded and murmured in agreement. I had no idea what was on the reel, but it seemed to carry significant importance. Perhaps it was some kind of local government announcement, or maybe a documentary relevant to Brazzaville's political situation. Whatever it was, it was now clear that the French crew was relying on this one film to fill a significant portion of the station's early airtime.

This was a far cry from what I had imagined. I had envisioned a station brimming with content from the moment we went live, a steady stream of programming that would captivate and inform viewers, bringing the wonders of television to Brazzaville in a grand spectacle. Instead, we had a single film reel and a production crew that seemed more interested in speaking among themselves than in planning the future of the station. There was a palpable disconnect between the ambition of what we were trying to achieve and the reality of the situation. The equipment was in place, the station was ready to broadcast, but there was almost nothing to put on air. And with the French crew showing no signs of urgency, I couldn't help but feel a growing sense of unease.

I stood there, watching as the government officials left the station, their task complete. The French crew, meanwhile, gathered around the

16mm reel, exchanging quiet remarks in their familiar French, seemingly unbothered by the fact that they had little else to work with. I could only hope that once this initial broadcast was made, they would begin to take things more seriously. After all, a television station isn't just about the equipment—it's about what you put on air.

But for now, it seemed we would be relying on that single reel of film, and I would be left wondering what, exactly, the French crew had in mind for the future of the station.

The Test Pattern

After weeks of effort, the station was finally taking shape, and my role had gradually shifted from hands-on installation to training and guidance. The French crew, for all their initial reluctance, were quick learners once they got past the unfamiliar English labels and the equipment's quirks. I continued with my training sessions, showing them how to handle the cameras, switch between feeds, and manage the control desk. Slowly but surely, I was able to step back and let them take the reins. It was a relief, in many ways, to see them gaining confidence in the operation of the station.

Meanwhile, my new friend, the French engineer, had been busy conducting field strength tests. He'd been out in the streets of Brazzaville for days, checking the transmitter's signal and ensuring that the coverage was strong and reliable. I hadn't seen much of him during this time, but he returned to the station one afternoon with a broad smile and a thumbs-up, a rare display of enthusiasm from a man who usually kept his emotions close to the chest. The transmitter, it seemed, was working perfectly, and the signal was reaching well beyond the city limits.

With everything in place, we began broadcasting a test pattern across Brazzaville. The test pattern—a simple image of concentric circles and a central marker, accompanied by a steady tone—was the first signal the station had ever sent out, and though it wasn't much to look at, it was a symbol of all the work we had put in. The image flickered onto the monitors, and I watched as the lines held steady, the signal crisp and clear.

Word spread quickly, and soon the government officials were making their way to the station, smiling broadly as they saw the test pattern on the screen. They didn't need to understand the technical details to know what it represented: progress. Even the local staff, who had been indifferent at first, began to show signs of excitement. There was a buzz in the air, a shared sense that we were on the verge of something significant.

The moment we had all been waiting for—the official opening ceremony—was scheduled for the next day. It was hard to believe we had finally made it. After weeks of sweat, setbacks, and the occasional misunderstanding, the station was ready to go live. There was still plenty to do, of course, but the hardest part was behind us. The signal was strong, the equipment was working, and the French crew had taken control of the operation.

That evening, we gathered at the French restaurant by the river, our unofficial headquarters for moments of celebration. The atmosphere was buoyant. The French production crew, who had once seemed so distant and reluctant, were now laughing and chatting with me like old friends. My French engineer colleague, his work now complete, was the star of the night, pouring wine with abandon and gesturing wildly as he recounted his adventures in the field, measuring signal strength across the city. The wine flowed freely, and the conversation followed suit. I even managed to keep up with some of the rapid French chatter, aided no doubt by the influence of the wine.

For the first time since I had arrived in Brazzaville, I allowed myself to relax. We had done it. The station was ready, and tomorrow we would flick the switch and bring television to this part of Africa for the very first time. As I sat there, glass in hand, I looked around the table at the people I had come to know over these past weeks. The early tensions, the cultural misunderstandings, and the technical challenges now seemed a distant memory. In their place was a sense of friendship and shared accomplishment.

Outside, the African night stretched overhead, vast and magnificent. Here in Brazzaville, there were few street lamps or other bright lights to soften the night sky. The darkness was deep, almost absolute, but with it came a breathtaking brilliance. The stars, freed from the interference of city lights, seemed closer, sharper, and more numerous than I had ever seen them. It was one of the many wonders of Africa, this sky alive with stars, a spectacle so vivid and clear that it felt like the heavens themselves were closer to the earth. I had seen many things during my time in Brazzaville, but nothing quite like the African night.

The Congo River rolled past in the twilight, its surface catching the last of the fading light. In the distance, the sounds of the city echoed faintly, a reminder of the world we were about to connect to something much larger. Tomorrow, Brazzaville would see its first broadcast, and the small group of us around the table would have made it happen.

As the night wore on and the wine continued to flow, there was a quiet sense of triumph among us. For all the hurdles, all the frustrations, we had brought something new into the world. And for that night, at least, everything seemed well.

The French Riviera of the Congo

As I settled into life in Brazzaville, with its mixture of the familiar and the unexpected, I began to uncover traces of the city's unique past —one that was shaped as much by colonial opulence as by the gritty work of establishing a new nation. From the moment I arrived, I'd been struck by certain peculiarities: the grand old hotels, the fine French restaurants, the cafés that could rival anything on the Champs-Élysées. All of these bore the remnants of a time when Brazzaville had been more than just a colonial outpost; it had been a prized destination for the French elite, a jewel set along the Congo River.

There was a time, before independence in 1960 I learned, when Brazzaville had been a coveted retreat for the wealthy, seeking exoticism without the rugged inconvenience of many far-flung colonies. While Parisian society braved the cold winters, the French in Brazzaville were living in a tropical paradise, with five-star hotels, breezy terraces, and gourmet cuisine to enjoy under the brilliant African sun. This was not the Brazzaville of independence struggles or political tensions but an earlier, glossier version of the city, one designed to entice the most discerning of French holidaymakers.

The hotels were grand, built in a style that

combined colonial grandeur with understated modernity. The architecture was distinctly European, but the environment—a wilderness at the city's edges, the vast Congo River flowing beside it—gave it an exotic air that would have made any Parisian swoon. Some of these hotels still operated, their worn façades showing glimpses of the luxury they once embodied. Even now, I could walk through the lobbies of places like the Hôtel de la Paix and imagine the elite gatherings that had once filled its halls, the laughter of French tourists mingling with the low hum of conversation.

In those days, Brazzaville had catered almost exclusively to the French. The cafés served freshly baked baguettes, the bars stocked fine French wines, and the menus boasted dishes more suited to the streets of Paris than to the heart of Africa. There were entire restaurants that existed solely to satisfy the French palate, places where local ingredients were transformed into French haute cuisine, much to the delight of the tourists who saw themselves as pioneers in a land far from home.

Jean-Claude, my ever-reliable colleague, spoke fondly of these days. "Brazzaville was the height of sophistication," he once told me, his voice tinged with nostalgia. "People came here to live a dream, a taste of Africa without the hardships."

He pointed out the palm-lined boulevards and manicured parks that had once been carefully maintained for the enjoyment of visitors. I learned that, in its heyday, Brazzaville had boasted luxury shopping, high-end art galleries, and even imported fabrics and perfumes to keep its guests in touch with the latest Parisian trends. For those seeking a thrill, safaris could be arranged with the greatest ease, allowing French tourists to dip their toes into the wilds of Africa before returning to the comforts of five-star luxury by nightfall.

But it wasn't just the hotels or the fine dining that had drawn the French to Brazzaville. It was also the sense of exclusivity, the knowledge that they were in an African oasis designed just for them. The French, who had left their mark on the city's infrastructure and culture, had built an enclave that gave them all the comforts of home with the added allure of the unknown. For the cost of a voyage and a week's stay, the average Frenchman could become an adventurer of sorts—sipping champagne on the hotel terrace while gazing out over the wild Congo River, the distant roar of unseen creatures in the air.

Yet, as independence swept across Africa, Brazzaville's role as a tourist haven for the French elite faded almost overnight. The luxurious hotels that had once been filled with well-dressed vacationers grew emptier, and the streets, once lined with imported cars and curious holidaymakers, slowly returned to the city's own rhythms. The French who had once made Brazzaville their private paradise drifted back to Europe, taking their tastes and wealth with them.

As I sat in the remnants of one such café, a place that still served its coffee in fine china, I couldn't help but imagine the city as it once was —a glamorous escape, a sanctuary for French holidaymakers, an African Tahiti where every detail was crafted to fit the colonial fantasy. It was an image of a Brazzaville that no longer existed, yet it lingered in the walls of these old hotels, in the dusty wine lists, in the faint echoes of French music that occasionally drifted from the bar.

This was the Brazzaville I'd never expected to find—a city whose past was as layered and complex as its present. It was a reminder that the world is rarely as straightforward as it seems, that the stories of places endure long after their eras have ended, woven into the fabric of everyday life. Brazzaville may have transformed, but echoes of its past remained, subtle reminders of a time when the city was a distant paradise for those who could afford to indulge in its luxuries.

As I prepared to leave, I realised that, in some way, I'd stumbled upon a version of Brazzaville that was as much a relic as the old hotels and the stately colonial buildings. The city had lived through many transformations, and I had been privileged to glimpse at least a few of them. And just like the colonial tourists who had come before, I, too, would leave with my own memories of this place—a mix of old and new, a place both foreign and familiar.

The Shadow of Politics

As the final preparations for the station's opening ceremony came together, the sense of accomplishment that filled the air was undeniable. We had overcome countless obstacles—technical, cultural, and logistical— to bring television to Brazzaville. But the momentous event was unfolding against a backdrop of political tension that simmered just beneath the surface.

It wasn't long before I heard the name David

Dacko mentioned in the hushed conversations of the local government officials who frequented the station. Dacko was not just another politician; he was the president of the Central African Republic, a neighbouring country whose political fortunes seemed inextricably linked to the turbulent post-colonial era. His story, like that of many African leaders at the time, was one of ambition, adversity, and the precarious balance of power in a newly independent nation.

Dacko had risen to prominence as the first president of the Central African Republic when it gained independence from France in 1960. The story of how he had come to power was well-known throughout the region. A protégé of his cousin, Barthelemy Boganda, the founding father of the nation, Dacko had been thrust into the spotlight following Boganda's untimely death in a plane crash. Dacko inherited not only his cousin's political mantle but also the immense challenges of leading a fledgling state. His vision had been clear: to elevate the standard of living for his people and to bring an end to the inter-tribal conflicts that plagued his country.

But the reality was far more complicated. Despite his early promises, Dacko struggled to stabilise the Central African Republic's failing economy, a challenge compounded by widespread corruption and economic mismanagement. His one-party rule, which initially seemed necessary to maintain order, eventually became a source of unrest.

Dacko's story weighed heavily on my mind as I considered the broader context of what we were doing in Brazzaville. While we were busy installing television transmitters and preparing to broadcast test patterns, the political landscape of Africa was shifting in ways that would have long-lasting repercussions. Here in Brazzaville, the political situation felt relatively stable for the moment, but the history of this region—especially the tumultuous events in nearby Central Africa—was a constant reminder that stability could be fleeting.

The officials who came to the station were outwardly cheerful about the progress we had made, but there was an underlying tension that I couldn't quite put my finger on. Perhaps it was the knowledge that, just across the border, leaders like Dacko were being toppled in coups, their regimes brought down by the same military officers who had once served them loyally. The Central African Republic's rich natural resources—diamonds, uranium, and other minerals—were coveted by many, but they had done little to lift the country out of poverty. Instead, these resources often fuelled corruption and further deepened the divide between the ruling elite and the impoverished masses.

David Dacko's fate was a constant reminder of how fragile power could be in this part of the world. He had risen quickly to the top, only to be toppled just as swiftly. And yet, remarkably, he would return to power again, years later, in another dramatic twist of political fate. His survival of assassination attempts and his ability to reclaim the presidency in 1979, only to be removed again by military force in 1981, mirrored the chaotic history of his landlocked nation—a country where political upheaval seemed to be the only constant.

As I worked alongside the French crew, making final adjustments to the equipment and ensuring everything was in place for the opening ceremony, I couldn't help but think about the broader implications of what we were doing. This television station, a small but significant piece of modern technology, would soon be broadcasting to a city and a country that were still grappling with the legacies of colonialism and the uncertain path of independence. What role would television play in shaping the political landscape of Brazzaville and beyond? Would it serve as a tool for education and progress, as Dacko had once hoped for his country, or would it become another instrument of power in the hands of those who controlled the airwaves?

The night before the opening ceremony, I stood outside the station, looking up at the sky. The stars were brilliant, as they always were in Brazzaville. Here, with so few streetlights and so little light pollution, the night sky seemed almost overwhelming in its clarity. The blackness of the African night was vast, but it was punctuated by the sharp, bright points of stars that felt impossibly close, as though you could reach out and touch them. It was a sight I had come to love, a reminder of the world beyond the daily challenges we faced here on the ground.

But beneath that starry sky, the realities of post-colonial Africa loomed large. Dacko's story was just one example of the struggles that newly independent nations were facing all across the continent. The future of Brazzaville, like that of so many other African cities, was uncertain. Television could be a powerful force for good, or it could become another tool in the hands of those who sought to control the narrative.

As we gathered that evening for a final meeting at the French restaurant, the wine and conversation flowed freely, much like the night before. But for me, there was a sense of gravity beneath the celebration. The opening of the station was a milestone, but it was also just the beginning. The political winds were shifting across Africa, and I wondered what role our station might play in those winds.

For now, though, all seemed well. Tomorrow would be a day of celebration, and Brazzaville would take its first step into the world of television broadcasting. What would come after, only time would tell.

The Broadcast Begins

The clock on the control room wall seemed to tick louder as the minutes inched closer to the transmission deadline. The air was thick with anticipation, a nervous tension that ran through everyone in the room—myself included. We had spent weeks building toward this moment, and now everything rested on the next few minutes. The French crew, who had once seemed reluctant and distant, were now fully engaged, their eyes glued to the equipment as they made their final adjustments. The station was ready.

The excitement around the station grew in the days leading up to the opening ceremony, and plans for the first live broadcast took shape quickly. Among the highlights of the evening was a scheduled performance by an African dance troupe—an arrangement that thrilled both the local government officials and the French crew, who were eager to showcase a piece of Brazzaville's culture to the newly connected viewers. I was equally intrigued; this would be my first time seeing such a performance up close, let alone broadcasting it live.

The troupe arrived in the early afternoon, and I remember spotting them outside the studio, rehearsing in a small clearing where they had space to move freely. The group was striking, dressed in colourful, traditional costumes that seemed to burst with life against the dusty backdrop of the studio lot. Their outfits were adorned with intricate beading, feathers, and vibrant cloths, each piece of clothing telling a story of its own. Many of the dancers carried spears, while others held tall drums, their hands resting lightly on the instruments as they prepared.

I watched from a distance at first, mesmerised by the way they moved. Even in rehearsal, there was a vitality to their movements, a kind of grace and strength that was entirely foreign to me. I had seen plenty of rehearsals before, but nothing like this. This was not just dance—it was storytelling, a display of history and culture that seemed to breathe life into the air around them.

As I approached, one of the dancers caught my eye and waved me over with a warm smile. They welcomed me into their circle, friendly and eager to share their world, despite the language barrier that separated us. They spoke in Lingala, and I could only respond with simple gestures, but there was a mutual understanding, a respect that didn't require words. I gestured to my camera, and, with a nod of approval, they posed for me, standing proudly in their costumes, spears held high, their faces bright with anticipation for the performance to come.

The light outside was perfect that afternoon, casting a soft glow over the group as they stood in formation, their traditional attire a burst of colour and texture against the simplicity of the studio's exterior. I snapped a few photos, capturing the intricate details of their costumes, the expressions of pride and joy on their faces. It was a rare privilege, and I knew that these photographs would be among the most cherished memories of my time in Brazzaville.

As the troupe continued their rehearsal, I noticed the way the drums set the rhythm, a deep, resonant beat that seemed to pulse through the ground. The dancers moved in perfect harmony with the rhythm, their steps powerful yet fluid, their movements echoing something ancient and timeless. I was reminded, in that moment, of how different this place was from London, where our dances were structured, our rhythms confined to set patterns. Here, there was freedom in the movement, a sense of connection to the land, to history, to one another.

Finally, as evening descended, the troupe gathered in the studio, waiting for their cue to perform live. The anticipation was palpable, both among the dancers and the crew. When the broadcast light turned on, the troupe sprang to life, filling the screen with movement, sound, and colour, their energy reaching out to every home tuned into the broadcast. It was a moment that needed no translation, a universal language of rhythm and movement that could be felt by anyone, anywhere.

The performance was a triumph, their movements flowing seamlessly from one sequence to the next, each dancer fully immersed in the rhythm. The drums echoed through the studio, filling the space with a sound that felt as old as the earth itself. Watching them on the monitor, I couldn't help but feel a sense of pride, knowing that we were bringing this piece of Brazzaville to the world, sharing its heartbeat with every viewer watching that night.

After the performance, the dancers exited the studio, grinning and breathless from the exertion, and gave me a nod as they left. I smiled back, a simple gesture of gratitude for a moment that had captured the essence of this place more than words ever could.

The photographs I took that day remain some of my favourite mementoes from my time in Brazzaville—a reminder not only of the beauty and vibrancy of the dance troupe but also of the spirit of the city itself, a place that welcomed me and shared its story with me, one rhythm at a time.

The single reel of film, carefully guarded for days, was finally unwrapped. It had been handled with an almost reverent care since its arrival, and now it was time for its moment in the spotlight. The French crew took their positions, threading the film onto the projector with precision. I stood back, watching them work, the hum of the machines blending with the quiet murmurs of French conversation. There was no more time for troubleshooting or second-guessing. Everything had been tested, every piece of equipment double-checked. All we could do now was press the button and let the broadcast begin.

With the film securely in place, the final countdown began. My eyes flicked to the monitor, where the test pattern still held steady, waiting to give way to the first official broadcast. The seconds stretched out, each one feeling longer than the last. Jean-Claude, standing nearby, gave me a quick nod, his expression one of quiet approval. He, like the rest of us, understood the significance of this moment. Brazzaville was about to enter a new era.

At exactly the scheduled time, the start button was pressed. The test pattern vanished from the screen, replaced by a flicker of black, and then the film began. The image was clear, the sound crisp. The station was live.

I watched as the familiar face of President David Dacko appeared on the screen, his voice carrying confidently through the speakers. The film, as it turned out, was a propaganda piece—a carefully crafted account of Dacko's recent diplomatic trip to France. It depicted a momentous occasion: the leaders of four nations within the French Community—formerly known as French Equatorial Africa—meeting with President Charles de Gaulle at the Élysée Palace in Paris. The purpose of the visit was to officially notify de Gaulle of their countries' desire for independence. The footage showed Dacko standing shoulder to shoulder with the other leaders, each of them a symbol of a new chapter in Africa's history. They were poised, diplomatic, and resolute as they met with de Gaulle, who listened with his characteristic sternness. The Elysee, grand and imposing, served as the backdrop for this historic meeting, where the future of these African nations was being forged. Dacko, in particular, appeared calm and statesmanlike as he addressed the cameras, speaking of his hopes for the Central African Republic and its path forward as an independent nation.

The narrative of the film was clear: these African leaders, including Dacko, were seeking a future beyond colonial rule, but they were doing so within the framework of the French Community. It was a delicate balance, one that acknowledged the influence of France while pushing for autonomy and self-determination. The tone of the film was celebratory, but also carefully controlled. It was, after all, a propaganda piece designed to present Dacko in the best possible light, reinforcing his position as a leader on the world stage.

As I watched the footage unfold, I couldn't help but reflect on the irony of it all. Here we were, broadcasting this film to the people of Brazzaville—a city and country grappling with its own post-colonial identity—on a station powered by British equipment, overseen by a British engineer, and staffed by a French production crew. It was a perfect encapsulation of the complex web of influences that defined this part of the world. French Equatorial Africa, now a collection of independent nations, still bore the marks of its colonial past, and leaders like Dacko were navigating that difficult transition with varying degrees of success.

The film continued, showing scenes of Dacko and his fellow leaders in discussion with de Gaulle, followed by shots of Paris—the grand boulevards, the majestic architecture, the symbols of French power and culture. It was clear that this broadcast was meant to reinforce the idea of a continuing bond between France and its former colonies, a relationship that remained deeply influential even as these nations sought to define their own futures.

The room was quiet as the film played on, the hum of the projector the only sound besides the narration coming through the speakers. I glanced around at the faces of the French crew. They seemed focused, intent on making sure the broadcast went smoothly, but there was no denying the political undertones that ran through the film. This was more than just a historical documentary—it was a message. A message about power, independence, and the ever-present shadow of colonial influence. As the film neared its end, the final scenes showed Dacko shaking hands with de Gaulle, their exchange framed as a moment of mutual respect and understanding. The camera lingered on Dacko's face, his expression one of determination as he looked toward the future. The message was clear: the Central African Republic, like the other nations of French

Equatorial Africa, was ready to step into the world as an independent nation, but it would do so with France's guidance still close at hand.

The film ended, the screen fading to black, and for a moment, the room was silent. Then, slowly, a ripple of applause spread through the control room. The broadcast had been a success. The first official transmission from the station had gone off without a hitch.

I leaned back in my chair, letting out a breath I hadn't realised I was holding. We had done it. Brazzaville's first television broadcast was in the books, and the station was officially on the air. What came next, no one could say for sure. But for now, we had made history.

A Visit to the President's Residence

In the aftermath of the successful first broadcast, a sense of accomplishment settled over the station like a warm, calming breeze. We had done it—brought television to Brazzaville for the very first time. The test pattern had transitioned into live broadcasting, and the single reel of film had delivered its message to the people. The opening ceremony had gone off without a hitch, and the hard work of the past few weeks was finally bearing fruit.

It wasn't long before word came that our efforts had not gone unnoticed. President David Dacko himself had invited the entire television station staff to a reception at his residence. The invitation came through Jean-Claude, who relayed the message with the same calm efficiency he had maintained throughout the project. We were all to attend, to be honoured for the role we had played in this momentous achievement.

The news sparked a quiet flurry of excitement among the French crew and the local staff. For many, it was a once-in-a-lifetime opportunity to meet the president, and the significance of the event wasn't lost on me either. Dacko was no ordinary leader; he was the first president of a newly independent nation, a symbol of post-colonial Africa's future. And now, we were about to stand in the same room as him, to be recognised for our part in ushering in a new era for Brazzaville.

The reception was held at a residence steeped in history. Brazzaville, after all, had once been the capital of "Free France" during World War II, and Charles de Gaulle had maintained his presence there during the conflict. The house we were invited to had been built for de Gaulle himself, a stately building that now served as the home of President Dacko. It was a reminder of the deep, lingering ties between France and this part of Africa, even as the region continued to forge its own identity.

When we arrived, the house stood grand and imposing, its colonial architecture still carrying echoes of the past. But now, it was a symbol of the present—of Dacko's leadership and his efforts to guide the country through the complex early years of independence. The atmosphere was formal, but there was a quiet warmth in the air as we were welcomed into the residence. Government officials, dressed in their finest, mingled with the station staff, and the soft murmur of French and Lingala drifted through the room.

Lunch was served in the expansive dining area, a spread of both French and local dishes that showcased the blending of cultures that defined Brazzaville. The French crew, no longer the aloof group that had arrived weeks before, seemed relaxed now, laughing and chatting easily. We had all worked hard to make the station a reality, and this reception felt like the perfect reward for our efforts.

After lunch, we were invited to step outside to the gardens, where a small podium had been set up. President Dacko arrived shortly after, making his entrance with a quiet dignity that commanded the attention of everyone present. He was dressed in flowing white robes that caught the light, a striking figure against the backdrop of the lush greenery. He moved with an air of authority, but there was also something approachable about him, a quality that set him apart from the more rigid political figures I had encountered in the past.

As Dacko made his way through the small crowd, shaking hands and exchanging words with the French crew and local officials, I watched with a sense of quiet awe. Here was the man whose image had filled the screen the day before, his presence commanding not just as a political leader, but as a symbol of the hopes and aspirations of a nation still finding its way.

When he reached me, I remember standing a little taller, unsure of what to expect. Dacko extended his hand, and I grasped it, feeling the firmness of his grip. He smiled warmly, speaking in French as he addressed me. Though I didn't catch all of his words, I understood the sentiment. He was thanking us—not just the crew, but me personally—for the work we had done to bring television to his country. For a moment, the language barrier didn't seem to matter. His appreciation was clear.

After the formalities, the real surprise came: we were to be awarded medals in recognition of our contributions to the project. It was an unexpected honour, and as each of us was called forward, I felt a deep sense of pride. Dacko himself presented the medals, pinning each one to our chests as we stood before him. When my turn came, I felt the weight of the small medallion settle against my chest—a tangible symbol of the work we had accomplished. It was a moment I knew I would carry with me long after I left Brazzaville.

As the afternoon wore on and the reception began to wind down, I found myself standing in the gardens, looking out over the grounds of the residence. The sky above was a deep, cloudless blue, and the warmth of the sun felt comforting. The significance of the moment wasn't lost on me. We had done more than just install a television station; we had contributed to a chapter of Brazzaville's history, however small our role may have been.

Dacko, still dressed in his flowing robes, moved among the guests with ease, a leader at home in his surroundings, yet aware of the weight of his position. His country faced immense challenges —economic struggles, political tensions—but for this one afternoon, there was a sense of calm, a sense of accomplishment. And for that, I was grateful to have been a part of it.

As we left the residence later that day, medals pinned to our chests, I couldn't help but reflect on how far we had come. From the dust and disarray of the early installation days to the polished ceremony of the opening broadcast, it had been a journey marked by both frustration and triumph. And now, standing on the threshold of a new era for Brazzaville, I couldn't help but feel that, in some small way, we had helped make history.

Into the Countryside

The day after our reception at President

Dacko's residence, I was invited on an outing into the countryside. Jean-Claude and the French engineer, my companions through many of the project's ups and downs, were taking me out for a drive. It was a welcome change from the hum of the station and the constant bustle of Brazzaville. I was eager to see more of the land beyond the city, imagining dense tropical jungles brimming with wildlife. After all, we were practically on the equator, and that's what I expected.

As we left the city behind, however, I was surprised to see that the landscape was nothing like I had imagined. There were no thick forests or jungles, no towering trees tangled in vines. Instead, we drove through vast open plains, stretching out as far as the eye could see—more reminiscent of the Australian outback than the tropical scenes I had envisioned. The sun hung high in the sky, casting long shadows across the flat, golden landscape, with occasional clusters of trees breaking the monotony.

For about an hour, we drove in comfortable silence, the three of us—Jean-Claude behind the wheel, the French engineer in the passenger seat, and me in the back, enjoying the open road. The car hummed along steadily, the countryside rolling by with a sense of quiet, undisturbed calm. It was a perfect day, the kind that seemed to stretch endlessly ahead.

At some point during the drive, I noticed a track branching off from the main road, leading up to a small hill in the distance. The hill was a modest rise in the otherwise flat landscape, and I felt an urge to stretch my legs, to walk to the top and take in the view. The thought of standing at the summit, looking out over the plains with my camera in hand, was irresistible.

"Can we stop here?" I asked Jean-Claude, leaning forward. "I'd like to walk up to the top of that hill and get some photos."

Jean-Claude glanced at me through the rearview mirror, and for a brief moment, there was a pause. Then, with a small shrug, he pulled over to the side of the road, slowing the car to a stop. I thanked him, opened the door, and stepped out into the warm, dry air.

Strangely, neither Jean-Claude nor the French engineer made any move to join me. They remained in the car, glancing at each other briefly before turning their attention back to the road ahead. I found it odd but didn't think too much of it at the time. They probably just wanted to relax, I told myself, and the idea of walking up a hill under the equatorial sun might not have seemed as appealing to them as it did to me.

Undeterred, I began making my way up the track, the grass crunching underfoot as I climbed toward the hilltop. The view grew wider with each step, the plains below unfurling in every direction like a vast, golden ocean. When I reached the top, I was greeted by an expansive, breathtaking panorama. The land stretched out endlessly, with nothing but sky and earth meeting at the horizon. It was a photographer's dream, and I took out my camera, snapping a few pictures as the wind swept softly across the hill.

After a few minutes of taking in the view, I began my descent, feeling refreshed and content. As I made my way back down toward the car, I noticed something odd. Both Jean-Claude and the French engineer were looking at me intently, their expressions tense, though they said nothing as I approached. Once I reached the car, they quickly beckoned me inside, gesturing for me to close the door behind me. Their apparent relief was palpable, though I couldn't quite understand why.

We drove off almost immediately, and the rest of the journey passed without incident. I didn't think to ask what had caused their strange behaviour—perhaps they were just worried about time or had some other engagement to attend to. Either way, I shrugged it off, still feeling satisfied from the outing and the views from the hilltop.

It wasn't until later that evening, back at the hotel, that I learned the full story. I was chatting with a fellow guest, a native English speaker who had lived in Brazzaville for some time, when I casually mentioned the hilltop stop. His eyes widened slightly, and he leaned in, lowering his voice as he spoke.

"You walked up that hill? Off the road, just like that?"

I nodded, a little confused by the sudden intensity in his tone.

"You're lucky, mate," he said, shaking his head. "Just a few weeks ago, some villagers were attacked and killed by lions on that very road. That area's been dangerous for a while. Didn't anyone tell you?"

For a moment, the words didn't quite sink in. Lions. The very road we had traveled on, the track I had walked up without a second thought. Suddenly, the strange behaviour of Jean-Claude and the French engineer made sense. They had known, of course—they must have—but for some reason hadn't told me, perhaps not wanting to alarm me or assuming I wouldn't take the risk. It was a chilling realisation, and I couldn't help but feel a shiver run down my spine as I imagined how close I might have come to danger.

Sitting there in the hotel, the reality of the situation washed over me. I had been walking in what I had thought was a peaceful, empty landscape, oblivious to the very real threats that lay hidden in the wild. The thought of lions roaming nearby, their presence unknown to me, added a layer of respect for the African countryside that I hadn't fully appreciated before.

From that point on, I knew I'd have to be more cautious, to respect the land in a way I hadn't before. Brazzaville and its surroundings, for all their beauty, held a danger that was not always immediately visible. And while I had been lucky that day, I knew I couldn't afford to take such risks lightly again.

The Long Journey Home

The time had come for me to start the long journey home. My work in Brazzaville was complete, and though I was eager to return, there was a bittersweet feeling as I prepared to leave behind the people and places that had become familiar over the past weeks. As is the custom here, departing visitors were given a proper send-off at the airport, and my friends insisted on accompanying me for one last farewell.

The airport was small and bustling with the energy of people coming and going, but it all felt surreal to me as I stood there, watching the DC-8 being refuelled on the tarmac. The sleek jet sat in the afternoon sun, its engines silent for the moment, but soon it would carry me far from Africa. The DC-8, a marvel of its time, was the first jet-powered airliner manufactured by McDonnell Douglas. Designed for long-haul flights, it had a range of 2,700 miles—enough to make the journey across continents. I admired its form, knowing that soon I would be on board, starting the long journey back to England.

Before that, though, there was one last ritual to observe. My farewelling friends—Jean-Claude, the French engineer, and several others I had worked with—insisted I have a drink with them at the airport bar. It was a custom, after all, to share one final toast before parting ways. We made our way to the bar, and I could feel the warmth of their company even as my mind began to turn toward the flight ahead.

The bartender greeted us with a knowing smile, sensing the occasion. My friends stood around me, their expressions calm, but there was a sense of quiet anticipation as the bartender mixed and poured my drink. I watched as the liquid swirled in the glass, golden and tempting. As the flight was called over the loudspeaker, I raised the glass, toasted my friends, and downed the drink in one swift motion. It was strong, much stronger than I had anticipated, but I smiled and thanked them nonetheless.

There were handshakes all around—firm, heartfelt ones, the kind that mark the end of something significant. I looked each of them in the eye, feeling a swell of gratitude for the friendships formed and the experiences shared. Then, with a final wave, I walked across the tarmac toward the waiting aircraft, the sun casting long shadows as I approached the DC-8.

It wasn't until I took my seat on the plane that it hit me—what exactly had been in that drink? My head felt heavy, and my eyelids drooped almost immediately. Within moments, I had fallen into a deep, dreamless sleep, completely oblivious to the world around me. I didn't wake until we reached Gabon, the first stop on the long flight home. The jolt of the landing brought me back to consciousness, but even then, I felt groggy, as if I had been under some sort of spell.

The flight was long, passing through Marseille before finally arriving in Paris. By the time we touched down at Charles de Gaulle Airport, the memories of Brazzaville already felt like they were beginning to blur around the edges, becoming distant, like a dream that fades upon waking.

In Paris, the PYE agent was waiting for me, just as planned. He was a tall, affable man with an easy smile, and his wife stood beside him, both of them eager to show me some Parisian hospitality before I continued on to London. They whisked me away from the airport, and we spent the evening enjoying the city in a way that seemed almost unreal after my time in Africa.

That night, they took me to the famous Crazy Horse Bar—a world away from the quiet, star-filled nights in Brazzaville. The lights, the music, the atmosphere—it was as if I had stepped into another world entirely. Paris, with its glamour and sophistication, seemed to swallow me whole, making the vast plains of Brazzaville feel even more distant. The contrast was striking, and for the first time, I realised how far I had come—not just in miles, but in experience.

The next day, after a comfortable night's sleep and a final Parisian breakfast, I boarded the flight to London for the final leg of my journey. I was struck by the quiet elegance of the Caravelle sitting there on the tarmac, having travelled on this aircraft many times before. Its sleek, all-metal frame gleamed under the airport lights, a symbol of the modern age. Unlike the lumbering propeller-driven aircraft of the past, the Caravelle seemed to belong to the future, its clean, swept-back wings and rear-mounted engines giving it an air of effortless grace. It was a far cry from the clunky machines of my youth.

The Caravelle was not just another airliner. It was a marvel of engineering, the kind of aircraft that whispered of progress. Its designers had learned from the tragic fate of the Comet, building thicker fuselage skins and more robust structural reinforcements, ensuring that the Caravelle would never suffer the same horrific failures. With its twin jet engines—at a time when four engines were still considered the norm—it was a bold step forward. The engines, mounted at the rear, not only gave the plane its distinctive silhouette but made it quieter than any other airliner in the sky. In fact, the noisiest seat on the Caravelle was said to be as quiet as the quietest seat on its rivals.

I sat down near the large, triangular window, noticing how its design, with its widely rounded corners, allowed just enough light to filter through while still offering a clear view of the world below. It was not simply an aesthetic choice, but a careful calculation for passenger comfort, one more example of the care and thought that had gone into this aircraft.

The Caravelle was capable of landing on all standard runways, and in the most difficult of conditions, it could deploy a tail parachute to shorten its landing distance. The pilots spoke of its 'kiss landings,' the large wings allowing it to glide down gently as though the very air itself welcomed its presence. It was said to be the first airliner in the world certified to make approaches with visibility as low as 50 feet—a feat unimaginable only a few years before.

The Caravelle's history was filled with stories that spoke of both daring and trust in its engineering. I remembered hearing about the time Air France had arranged a publicity stunt, gliding a Caravelle without propulsion for over 262 kilometres, restarting the engine only on the final approach. It was a demonstration of the plane's reliability, meant to quell any fears of jet travel. It worked. Within just a few years of its debut, the Caravelle had no rivals, with over 170 models sold to airlines around the world. As I looked out the window, the hum of the Rolls-Royce engines filling the cabin with their steady, muted sound, I realised how far the world had come since I was that twelve-year-old boy, straining to hear the faint signals from Brazzaville on our neighbour's radiogram. Now, here I was, crossing continents in the comfort of a machine that barely seemed to touch the air.

The Caravelle wasn't just an aircraft; it was a symbol of an era where technology promised to bridge the vast distances of the world, making it feel just a little bit smaller.

By the time we reached London, my African adventure felt like a distant memory, but I knew it would never truly leave me. It was a chapter of my life defined by a landscape as wild as the lions that roamed it, by a people who had embraced modernity while wrestling with the ghosts of their colonial past, and by the delicate balance between tradition and progress. And now, sitting aboard this sleek, futuristic aircraft, I could see how the world I was returning to had also changed in ways I was only beginning to understand.

As the plane ascended into the clouds, I thought back over my time in Africa. The people I had met, the challenges we had overcome, and the lessons I had learned. It had been an adventure unlike any other—a journey that had taken me far from home and taught me more than I could have ever imagined.

Brazzaville already felt like a memory, but it was a memory I would carry with me for the rest of my life. The sprawling plains, the star-filled nights, the friendship with the French crew, and the weight of history in every step—it was a chapter I would never forget.

As the plane descended toward London, I felt a strange mix of emotions—relief, nostalgia, and perhaps a little sadness. My African adventure had come to an end, but the stories, the images, and the people would stay with me, shaping the way I saw the world from that day forward.

I stepped off the plane, back in England, but a part of me was still in Brazzaville, under the vast African sky, where the past and future seemed to meet in a place that felt timeless.

Chapter 15: An Anecdote

As my departure from Brazzaville drew near, I thought it wise to send a message ahead to my manager back in London. After all, it had been some time since I'd checked in, and it seemed only sensible to inform him that I'd soon be returning, hopefully with some measure of success to report. I turned to Jean-Claude, who had proven himself invaluable as a guide through the labyrinthine world of post-colonial Brazzaville, and asked if there was a Telex machine I might use.

He looked at me with a puzzled expression. The French had brought modern communication equipment to Brazzaville in the past, yes, but when independence had been granted, most of those French communication experts had packed up and taken their equipment back to France with them. Telex machines, it seemed, were a rare commodity here, and finding a working one might prove a challenge. Nevertheless, he promised to make inquiries.

After a day of back-and-forth with various officials, Jean-Claude returned with news. There was, in fact, a functioning Telex machine, but it was housed at the African military base on the outskirts of Brazzaville, well within the heart of their heavily guarded headquarters. Using it would require a security clearance and an escort through the base—a task laden with enough red tape to make even the most bureaucratic office in London look streamlined by comparison.

At last, with the necessary permissions in hand, I was ushered into the military compound, a forbidding cluster of buildings that loomed with the seriousness of an institution unused to civilian presence. A uniformed officer led me down a series of dimly lit corridors, their concrete walls echoing with the distant sounds of radios and footsteps. Eventually, we reached a small room buried in the bowels of the building, and there, sitting in the centre, was the Telex machine.

The machine itself was a relic, worn but operational, its keys yellowed with age, each character faintly rubbed from the passing years. I was introduced to the operator, a young man who spoke only French, and we went through the slow process of preparing my message. I dictated in English, spelling out each word deliberately, letter by letter, and he transcribed in a language he likely didn't understand. It was a painfully tedious process, each letter laboriously typed as I enunciated it. Still, after what felt like an eternity, my message was finally sent: a brief note to my manager in London, advising him of my return.

With the message sent, I felt a sense of accomplishment, albeit a small one. I was on my way home, and my manager would be informed, even if he might have to wait a day or two for the message to actually arrive.

Days later, when I returned to London, rested and ready to report, I sought out my manager to greet him and, naturally, asked if he had received my Telex. He looked puzzled for a moment, as if trying to recall something half-remembered. I could tell from his expression that he hadn't the faintest idea what I was talking about. Seeing my confusion, he suggested I check with the office in the basement where our own Telex machine was housed.

Curious and a bit annoyed, I made my way down to the basement, the scent of dust and ink hanging thick in the air. There, sitting on the Telex machine, was my message, still waiting, untouched. It had only arrived a few hours earlier—days after I'd sent it—and no one had yet thought to check.

I could only shake my head and chuckle at the irony. I had gone through untold efforts to send a simple note, navigating military clearances and security escorts, only for it to languish in our own office, unseen and unread. My manager, who had barely raised an eyebrow when I'd mentioned it, laughed with me, a wry grin spreading across his face.

In the end, my telex message had served as little more than an exercise in patience. Yet it seemed a fitting conclusion to my time in Brazzaville—a reminder that, in a world changing as swiftly as ours, some messages would always take their time, no matter how advanced the machinery behind them.

A London Tale

In the early winter of 1962, amidst the charm of a West Kensington terrace house, destiny unfolded its script for an enduring love story. Patricia, my future wife, stood at the threshold of that Victorian doorway, her presence a timeless blend of grace and allure.

The air carried the sweet fragrance of autumn leaves as I approached, the click of my shoes echoing on the cobblestone path. Patricia, wrapped in a houndstooth coat, greeted me with a smile that mirrored the warmth within the quaint terrace. The air hummed with the melodies of a vinyl record playing inside, setting the tone for a serendipitous encounter. As we stepped into the drawing-room adorned with vintage wallpaper and plush furniture, the ambience exuded a sense of familiarity. The glow of a fireplace flickered, casting a dance of shadows on the walls. Conversation flowed effortlessly, weaving through tales of aspirations and shared curiosities. Patricia's laughter, like the crackling of the fireplace, echoed through the room.

The evening unfolded like a well-choreographed dance, each moment a step towards an unknown future. We found ourselves on the terrace, surrounded by the soft glow of lanterns and the distant hum of city life.

The stars above bore witness to the genesis of a connection that transcended the constraints of time. In Patricia's eyes, I glimpsed a reflection of dreams yet to be realised, and her words painted a canvas of possibilities. The terrace house in West Kensington became the cocoon where our hearts resonated in harmony, and the apple-blossom charm she carried seemed to infuse the very air we breathed.

Little did we know, amidst the Victorian

elegance and the autumnal embrace, that the terrace house in West Kensington had become the setting for a love story that would withstand the test of decades, an indelible chapter in the book of our shared history.

A Brush with Fame

It was early 1963, and I was working at a television studio housed in the Granville Theatre in London. The task at hand was to record a poetry reading by the inimitable Richard Burton, who was to breathe life into the words of Dylan Thomas. It promised to be an affair dripping with the kind of gravitas that could make a grown man weep.

The studio was buzzing with anticipation. Our small audience, a select few invited for this rare treat, included none other than Elizabeth Taylor herself. There she was, seated in the front row, her leg encased in a plaster cast—a remnant of a mishap on the set of Cleopatra. Even with that cumbersome cast, she radiated an allure that was almost palpable, a beacon of Hollywood glamour amidst our humble British setting.

As a humble technician, my role was far from the limelight. I was tasked with the less glamorous, though no less vital, job of ensuring our cameras operated without a hitch. But fate, it seemed, had other plans for me that day. Armed with a coil of camera cable, I concocted a flimsy excuse to be in the right place at the right time.

I saw my opportunity as Burton prepared to start his reading. I needed to adjust the camera angle—well, that's what I told myself. With my coil of cable, I manoeuvred myself between Elizabeth Taylor and Richard Burton. For a split second, I was in the presence of greatness, my heart pounding louder than Burton's recitation.

In a moment of sheer bravado, or perhaps folly, I turned and smiled at Elizabeth Taylor. And then it happened. I could swear she winked at me. Elizabeth Taylor, the goddess of the silver screen, acknowledging my existence! My mind raced with the possibilities—perhaps this was the start of my Hollywood career. I envisioned myself rubbing shoulders with the stars, attending glamorous parties, and receiving an Oscar for Best Cable Handling.

But alas, my dreams of Tinseltown glory were abruptly cut short. From the control room above, my future wife was watching. She had a keen eye and a sharper intuition. The fleeting wink from Taylor didn't escape her notice, nor did my sheepish grin. As I made my way back to my station, the cable coil feeling heavier by the second, I could almost feel her eyes boring into the back of my head.

Thus ended my brief brush with fame. Richard Burton continued with his reading, Elizabeth Taylor remained the queen of Hollywood, and I returned to my cables, my Hollywood dreams dashed—but with a story to tell.

The President's Visit

June 1963, a time of great excitement and even greater precipitation. President John F. Kennedy was visiting Ireland, and my employer, PYE TVT, had magnanimously offered a fully equipped and manned outside broadcast van to Teilifís Éireann to assist in the television coverage. Our van was set up near the Áras an Uachtaráin, the official residence of President Éamon de Valera, in the verdant expanse of Phoenix Park. Little did we know, we were in for a drenching experience that would leave us longing for the relative dryness of a fish tank.

It rained almost the entire time we were there. Not just a gentle drizzle, mind you, but a torrential downpour that seemed determined to soak us to the skin and beyond. Our task was to lay out camera cables across the wet grass, which quickly turned into a slippery, mud-splattered ordeal. We sloshed about, trying to avoid looking like bedraggled otters, but with little success. The highlight of our soggy endeavour was to be a tree-planting ceremony involving both Presidents. The plan was simple: wait for a miraculous pause in the rain, dash outside, and capture the historic moment for TV viewers worldwide. It sounded straightforward enough, but the weather had other ideas. After what felt like an eternity of waiting, huddled under makeshift shelters that did little to keep us dry, the rain finally eased. A flurry of activity ensued as both Presidents were ushered outside, shovels at the ready. We sprang into action, cameras rolling, trying to look professional despite our waterlogged state.

President Kennedy, ever the picture of charisma, managed to appear effortlessly dapper even as the drizzle resumed. President de Valera, with his stately bearing, seemed equally unfazed by the weather. They planted the tree with smiles and handshakes, the picture of diplomatic poise, while we captured every moment, hoping our equipment wouldn't short-circuit in the damp. As soon as the ceremony concluded and the Presidents retreated to the dry comfort of the Áras an Uachtaráin, the skies opened up once more with renewed vigour. We embarked on the exhausting task of packing up, slipping and sliding in the mud, and attempting to dry out our equipment and ourselves.

Once everything was finally stowed away, we faced the daunting prospect of moving our soggy selves and gear to Galway for the next day's reception at Eyre Square. But that, as they say, is another story. For now, we took solace in the knowledge that we had played our part in a historic moment, even if it meant being more soaked than a tea biscuit in a toddler's cup.

The Wall

It was August 1963, and the weather was kind, as if to soften the hard edges of the world around me. I arrived at the Hauptbahnhof Berlin after a long trip from Munich, weary and uncertain. The air of the city felt dense with the echoes of history and recent events—Kennedy's voice still seemed to reverberate from the walls, his declaration, "Ich bin ein Berliner," a defiant echo against the oppressive silence that divided East and West.

At 23, I was travelling alone, and Berlin's streets were strange and unsettling, like the corridors of a house in which I did not belong. Despite my unease, I made my way to Checkpoint Charlie, or "Checkpoint C," the infamous crossing point where the city's lifeblood seemed to freeze. The sight of the Wall, stretching endlessly, rough and imposing, made me shiver. I walked alongside it, tracing my fingers over its cold, impersonal surface, feeling the weight of a divided world press down upon my shoulders.

I was bound for the Hook of Holland, where the Harwich ferry awaited, but the journey required more than a simple ticket. To leave West Berlin, I had to obtain a special visa that necessitated a journey into East Berlin by train —a prospect that filled me with a quiet dread.

With every step, it felt as though I was crossing not just a physical boundary but some invisible line between freedom and the unknown.

After securing the visa, my relief was palpable. I hurried back to the Hauptbahnhof, my heart pounding, and boarded the next westbound train. This train, with its worn seats and the faint scent of distant places, had clearly travelled from deep within the eastern regions of Europe. It was full, yet I found a seat among a family group. Though we shared no common language, they welcomed me with gentle smiles and gestures. They offered me food from their modest supply, and in that moment, the fear and uncertainty seemed to recede, replaced by the simple warmth of human kindness.

As we rolled westward through Germany and on to Holland, I felt, for the first time in days, a flicker of hope, like the faintest glimmer of dawn after a long, cold night.

The Greyhound Bus

Ah, 1964—what a year to embark on a grand American adventure! My newlywed wife and I, armed with nothing but our Australian and Irish accents, and a pair of shiny new wedding rings, decided to conquer the vast landscape of the United States. The weapon of choice? A $99 Greyhound bus ticket that promised 99 days of unlimited travel. The catch? We needed foreign passports, which we had, and a sense of humour, which we definitely needed.

We set off from Toronto, Canada, brimming with excitement and clutching our suitcases like they were filled with gold rather than crumpled clothes. The Greyhound bus, a metallic behemoth of American engineering, awaited us with open doors. The driver, a grizzled veteran with a penchant for chewing tobacco, glanced at our tickets and muttered, "Tourists, eh? Good luck."

It was 1964, the sweltering heat of a New York summer hanging heavy in the air as my wife and

I stepped off the Greyhound from Toronto. The bus ride was but the first leg of our journey back to Australia, and yet here we were, bags in hand at the Port Authority Terminal, New York City looming large and indifferent around us. We'd decided to stay a week to see the World's Fair, that beacon of modernity and progress that seemed to promise glimpses of a future unfathomable back home.

The fairground was a world unto itself, glittering in steel and glass, brimming with excitement and pride in human ingenuity. We went back several times, unable to absorb all of it in a single visit. But there was one pavilion that left an indelible mark on me: the IBM pavilion. I'd heard of computers in vague terms, but this was my first encounter with their power. The character-recognition exhibit was, for me, pure magic. They handed each visitor an IBM card, a small piece of cardboard upon which one wrote a date – any date from the past century. You'd feed it to the machine, a hulking apparatus connected to an IBM 1311 Disk

Storage Drive, which then processed it through an IBM 1460 system, located remotely at the IBM computing section. Within seconds, it printed out the most significant headline from that date, spitting it out at an astonishing rate of 1,100 lines per minute. The precision and speed were overwhelming. It felt, in that instant, like the future had arrived. Here was a machine, coolly electronic, yet somehow close to possessing memory, almost human in its recall. My wife and I had come for the World's Fair, drawn by its shimmering vision of the future. But it was the city itself that captivated us, with its endless streets and a restless pulse we'd never quite experienced before. Between visits to the Fair's gleaming pavilions, we spent our afternoons wandering Manhattan, often carried along by the crowds, swept into New York's strange and lively embrace.

One afternoon, we found ourselves at the doors of Radio City Music Hall in Rockefeller Center, its Art Deco grandeur looming as if to challenge the city's own frenetic energy. We ventured inside for an afternoon performance, where the darkened theatre offered a brief respite, its grand interior whispering of elegance from another era. There, in the cool, hushed space, we could feel the vast machinery of the city slow down, if only for a moment, as if we'd glimpsed another side to New York—a place of opulence and refinement, suspended above the clamour outside.

Afterwards, we strolled down Broadway, passing Birdland, where a bold, black-and-white billboard proclaimed "Miles Davis—Tonight." Miles was more than a musician to me; he was an idol. I carried my Milestones record, bought fresh in London two years earlier, like a talisman. The idea of seeing him live was a dream, yet as dusk settled, we hesitated. Stories of city crime floated ominously around us, and the thought of braving public transport back into Broadway at night seemed, in the end, unwise. It felt faintly absurd to turn away, but that was New York in '64—electric and full of possibility, yet always tempered by shadows lying just beyond the bright lights.

Our next destination was Miami, the land of sunshine, beaches, and retirees in Bermuda shorts. The journey south was an eye-opener, filled with an eclectic mix of fellow travellers. There was an aspiring country singer who serenaded us with off-key ballads and a chatty grandmother who insisted on showing us photos of her seventeen grandchildren. By the time we reached Miami, we felt like seasoned voyagers, albeit with a slight ringing in our ears. Miami was a whirlwind of sandy toes and sunburnt noses. We revelled in the tropical paradise, sipping on cocktails that were far too strong for our delicate sensibilities. But soon enough, the Greyhound beckoned, and we were off again, this time headed westward to Los Angeles.

Crossing the country by bus is no small feat. It's a marathon of rest stops, roadside diners, and questionable motel rooms. We witnessed the majestic beauty of the Grand Canyon, the kitschy allure of Route 66, and the endless flatness of the Texan plains. Each new state brought its own flavour of Americana, from cowboy hats to Elvis impersonators. We even made friends with a pair of German backpackers who were just as bewildered by American portions as we were.

Arriving in Los Angeles felt like reaching the promised land. The city buzzed with Hollywood glamour, surfers, and smog. Our grand tour was nearing its end, but not before we boarded a passenger-carrying cargo ship destined for Australia. The ship was a floating menagerie of goods and passengers, where crates of bananas rubbed shoulders with honeymooners like us.

As we sailed away, leaving the Greyhound buses and the vast American highways behind, we couldn't help but laugh at the absurdity and brilliance of our journey. We had travelled over 5000 miles, met countless characters, and seen a lifetime's worth of sights. And all for $99—talk about a bargain!

A Passage to Singapore

In the summer of 1964, my newlywed wife and I embarked on a remarkable sea voyage aboard the M/V Ferncliff, a Norwegian diesel-powered cargo ship with a storied history. Built in 1955, the vessel exuded a sense of rugged charm, featuring comfortable and spacious cabins on the upper deck, providing a home away from home for a maximum of 12 passengers. Our maritime adventure began in the bustling port of Los Angeles, setting sail on a journey that would take us across the vast Pacific Ocean to the enchanting shores of Singapore. The route included captivating stops in Manila, Hong Kong, and Bangkok, each city leaving an indelible mark on our memories.

The eclectic mix of passengers on board added a unique dimension to our sea-bound escapade. A pair of American missionaries, bound for The Philippines, shared their tales of faith and service during the long days at sea. In Manila, we welcomed another intriguing duo—a husband and wife who dazzled with their magical performances and were en route to Bangkok to share their talents. As the Ferncliff cut through the Pacific waves, we encountered the unpredictability of the open sea. A malfunction in the ship's engines created a brief moment of suspense, emphasising the vulnerability of our vessel in the vastness of the ocean. However, the skilled crew swiftly addressed the issue, restoring our confidence in the sturdy Norwegian cargo ship. Hong Kong greeted us with unexpected intensity as a typhoon struck while we were anchored in the harbour. The swirling winds and torrential rain painted a dramatic picture against the city's skyline. The ship's crew adeptly navigated the challenges, providing us with a firsthand experience of the raw power of nature at sea.

Nights on the Ferncliff were a spectacle of lights, with distant vessel passing in the darkness. The rhythmic sound of waves against the ship's hull accompanied our reflections on the vastness of the ocean and the shared friendship among the passengers. The voyage was not merely a means of transportation; it was a canvas painted with unique and unexpected moments. Upon reaching the vibrant city-state of Singapore, our sea adventure concluded, and we transitioned to the swift luxury of a BOAC COMET jetliner. The flight, which included a stopover in Darwin, took us from the maritime serenity of the Ferncliff to the modern skies, offering a breathtaking perspective of the journey we had undertaken.

As we touched down in Sydney, the memories of our sea voyage lingered — a tapestry woven with the threads of diverse companions, dramatic challenges, and the boundless beauty of the open ocean. The M/V Ferncliff had been more than a mode of transport; it was the vessel that carried us through a transformative chapter in our lives, marking the beginning of our journey as a married couple.

The Apollo Moon Mission

In the late 1960's, my life took an extraordinary turn. It was 1967 when I came across an advertisement in the Melbourne Age that would change everything. NASA was seeking technical staff for its newly constructed tracking station at Honeysuckle Creek, south of Canberra. The thought of being part of the Apollo Moon Mission was irresistible, and I knew I had to seize the opportunity.

I prepared meticulously for the interview, excitement building as I realised what was at stake. They were looking for someone with technical expertise who was willing to work in a remote location. The position was for a data and telemetry engineer in the computer section, a role that promised to be both challenging and rewarding. After a rigorous selection process, I was thrilled to receive the offer. With my bags packed and heart full of anticipation, I set off for Honeysuckle Creek. Nestled in a picturesque valley surrounded by rolling hills and dense bushland, the tracking station felt like a world unto itself. It was remote and serene, yet buzzing with the excitement of scientific endeavour. My role involved working with large mainframe computers, my first experience with such technology. I was tasked with monitoring and analysing telemetry data from the Apollo spacecraft, ensuring smooth communication with mission control in Houston. It was a daunting responsibility but one that filled me with immense pride.

Working at Honeysuckle Creek was both challenging and immensely rewarding. The work was demanding, with long hours and high stakes, but the sense of purpose and teamwork made it all worthwhile. I was surrounded by highly qualified NASA engineers, and being embedded with them gave me a thorough grounding that would benefit me for years to come. We were a close-knit group, united by our shared mission and the unique nature of our location.

The job came with its share of heartbreak. In 1967, not long after I joined the team, disaster struck. During a routine test, a fire broke out in the Apollo 1 command module, killing astronauts Gus Grissom, Ed White, and Roger B. Chaffee. The news was devastating, casting a sombre shadow over our work. The tragedy underscored the perilous nature of our mission and the high stakes involved. Yet, amidst the grief, there was a steely determination to honour the fallen astronauts by pressing forward and achieving the goal they had worked so hard for. The sense of purpose that followed this setback was palpable. We were more focused than ever, determined to see the mission through. Every success and breakthrough felt like a tribute to the astronauts we had lost. The work with the large mainframe computers was a key part of this effort. These machines, which were the backbone of our operations, processed vast amounts of data and ensured that the astronauts' vital signs and spacecraft systems were continuously monitored. Mastering their use was both a challenge and a privilege.

One of the most memorable moments was the Apollo 11 mission in 1969. As Neil Armstrong and Buzz Aldrin prepared to land on the Moon, the atmosphere at the station was electric. We knew the world was watching, and the pressure was immense. I was on duty the night of the landing, and I can still recall the tension and excitement in the room. When Armstrong's voice crackled over the radio, announcing, "The Eagle has landed," a wave of relief and elation swept through us. We had done it; we were part of history. The isolation of Honeysuckle Creek could be tough at times. We often missed our families and the comforts of home, but the sense of purpose and the knowledge that we were contributing to something monumental kept us going. We were pioneers in a new frontier, and that was something truly special. The experience left a lasting impact on me. It taught me the value of teamwork, dedication, and perseverance. We were part of a global effort, a testament to what humanity could achieve when we worked together towards a common goal. Even now, years later, I look back on those days with a sense of pride and nostalgia. Honeysuckle Creek might have been a small, remote tracking station, but its role in the Apollo Moon Mission was significant. We were the unsung heroes behind the scenes, ensuring that the astronauts had the support they needed to explore the unknown. And in doing so, we helped to write a remarkable chapter in the history of space exploration.

Downsizing

Sitting in my room at the nursing home, I realise that everything I own is now contained within these four walls. It's a strange thought, really. If I had to pack it all up, it would easily fit into two large suitcases. The few clothes I have left, the handful of books, and some personal items—all of it could be packed away in a matter of hours.

It wasn't always like this. Not so long ago, I had a large house. A sprawling property with rooms I rarely used, and a garden that seemed to stretch on forever. There were two cars parked in the driveway, each serving its purpose, although one often just sat there, gathering dust. Then, there was the small yacht moored on Sydney Harbour. It was more of a status symbol than anything else, really. I liked the idea of owning a yacht, even if I only sailed it a handful of times each year.

The garage was another story altogether. It was stacked high with unlabelled cartons, each one filled with things I thought I might need someday. Tools I never used, old furniture that had been replaced but not discarded, and boxes of memorabilia from years gone by. It was all just sitting there, taking up space. I even had to rent a storage facility nearby to house the overflow. The things I couldn't fit in the garage but couldn't bear to part with.

And now, all of that is gone. The house, the

cars, the yacht, the garage full of stuff—all of it has been sold, given away, or simply left behind. I'm left with the essentials, the bare minimum. It's a strange feeling, knowing that everything I once valued so highly has been reduced to what could be carried in a couple of suitcases. But this is my reality now, and I suppose there's a kind of simplicity in that.

Peace

The room is quiet now. The carers came early, as they always do. They tidied up, fussed over the bed, straightened the pillows, and left me with a soft smile. It's a small room but tidy, everything in its place. The morning light is coming through the window, and there's a promise of a fine day ahead. The air smells fresh, and the birds are starting their usual chatter outside. I let my breakfast settle—just tea and toast today—and sit back in my chair, watching the light shift on the wall.

There's a kind of peace in the morning, before

the nursing home stirs too much. The nurses make their rounds, gentle and quick, like they've done this a thousand times. They check on us, ask how we're feeling, and go about their way, always with a kind word. There are activities planned for later—nothing too strenuous. I might join in, or I might not. I'll decide when the time comes. I hear the front doors creak, and a few of the relatives start to arrive. Some look cheerful, but I see the tears in their eyes, even if they try to hide them. We all pretend not to notice. That's how it is. We don't talk about the sadness much. I don't mind the company, though. I've learned to take the day as it comes.

For now, I just sit here. The day stretches ahead of me, simple and calm. I've no need to rush. There's a stillness in the air, and I breathe it in. The sun is getting warmer, the world outside moving along. It's a good day, I think. Better than most.

At 84, the world looks smaller. Life is quieter,

and the noise that once filled the days— ambition, expectation, even fear—has faded. I sit here with few possessions. A chair, a bed, a handful of books, and the memories. There was a time when I thought I needed more. A bigger house, more money, more success. Now, I see those things for what they were —temporary distractions.

Should I have done things differently? That's the question, isn't it? I think about it often. Not with regret, but with the kind of clarity that comes when you've lived through the storms and come out the other side. I think of the people I loved, and the ones I let go of too soon. There are a few faces that haunt me still. I wonder what my life would've been like if I'd stayed close to them, or if I'd been braver in telling them how much they meant. I spent too much time chasing things that don't matter now. Money slips through your fingers, and success fades faster than you expect. But time, once it's gone, never comes back. Perhaps I should have spent more of it with the ones who loved me, should've lingered longer in the moments that mattered. But there's no sense in wishing for the past to change. I am here, with what I have, and maybe that's enough. Life is what it is, and I can't say it's been unkind to me. If I have any regret, it's that I didn't realise sooner what truly mattered. But then again, who ever does? You live, you learn, and eventually, you let it all go. That's the way of it.

It is a strange thing, the way society treats its elders, as though age itself were an affliction to be avoided at all costs. We parade the young and the vigorous before us, celebrating their energy and ambition, while quietly shuffling the old to the margins, as if their time had passed and they had nothing more to offer. But this, like so many assumptions we hold, is not only cruel but deeply mistaken.

For there was a time, not so long ago, when age was seen as a badge of honour. The older generation, having weathered the storms of life, were respected not in spite of their years, but because of them. The wrinkles on their faces, the slow stoop of their backs— these were the marks of wisdom hard- earned, lessons learned in a world where survival was not guaranteed. They had known hardship, sacrifice, and perseverance in ways the young cannot yet comprehend.

Yet now, in our frantic chase after youth, we have forgotten the value of experience. We treat the elderly as though they were a burden— shutting them away in homes, dismissing their opinions as "out of touch," and pretending, all the while, that we shall never grow old ourselves. In our self- absorption, we have stripped them of the very dignity they deserve.

The truth is that age demands our respect, not our pity. For it is the older generation who have laid the foundations upon which we now build our lives. Without their labour, their resilience, we would have nothing. And what a bitter irony it is that those who have given us everything are now treated as though they have nothing left to give.

The measure of a society, it has often been said, lies in how it treats its weakest members. I would add that its soul is revealed in how it honours those who came before. If we cannot respect the old, then we are no better than animals.

The Slow Lane

As I shuffle down the corridor of the nursing home, the familiar scent of disinfectant and the faint hum of fluorescent lights envelops me. The carpeted floor echoes with the soft squeak of my worn-out slippers, each step a reminder of the passage of time. This place has become my home, a place where the ticking clock on the wall seems to keep pace with the rhythm of my heartbeat.

I find solace in the routine, the carefully orchestrated series of events that dictates my days. Breakfast is served promptly at 8:00 a.m., a warm bowl of oatmeal accompanied by a cup of strong coffee. The dining room buzzes with conversations, a symphony of stories, laughter, confusion, and the occasional tear. Faces, once strangers, have become characters in the ongoing saga of our lives.

The days are marked by activities designed to fill the hours with purpose. Bingo games and chair exercises replace the hustle and bustle of the outside world. We have become a community, bound by the shared experience of ageing and the need for companionship in the face of solitude.

As the sun dips below the horizon, casting its long shadows through the windows, the mood in the nursing home shifts. It is a time when memories of the past creep in, uninvited but somehow welcomed. The quiet corridors become a canvas upon which the stories of our lives unfold. I often find myself wandering through the dimly lit hallways, pausing at the framed photographs that adorn the walls—frozen moments capturing the vitality of youth, a stark contrast to the reality of our present.

Loneliness has become a constant companion, but within the walls of the nursing home, a sense of friendship has blossomed. We forge connections, form alliances, and lean on each other to navigate the challenges that come with ageing. The staff, with their tireless dedication, have become our extended family, providing comfort and care in the absence of our own families.

As the night descends, I retreat to my room, its modest furnishings a testament to a frugal life well-lived. The bed, once a symbol of rest and rejuvenation, now cradles the weariness of countless nights. I stare at the ceiling, a canvas of dreams and regrets, wondering what stories it holds within its silent expanse.

In the solitude of my room, I reflect upon the journey that has led me to this place. Life in the nursing home is a delicate dance between acceptance and resilience. It is a tapestry woven with threads of joy, sorrow, and an unwavering human spirit. Though the days may blur into one another, each holds a unique chapter in the story of our shared existence.

Brief Encounters

Living in a nursing home has brought a mix of emotions, offering a unique perspective on life. The routine here is steady, and the days tend to blend into each other. Yet, amidst the routine, the unexpected arrival of friends and relatives visiting the other residents, brings a welcome change.

I vividly recall the initial encounters with these visiting kinfolk – warm smiles and genuine conversations that broke the monotony of the nursing home ambiance. Their visits injected a fresh vibrancy into my days, making the time spent more enjoyable. As we shared stories and laughter, it felt like a brief escape from the routine. Among the visitors, I formed a particularly special connection with more than one person. We discovered common interests and shared experiences that transcended the generational gap. The friendship blossomed effortlessly, becoming a source of joy and companionship during their visits. Our time together brought a sense of belonging, a feeling that transcended the institutional setting of the nursing home.

However, as abruptly as these connections formed, they disintegrated. The visiting relatives stopped coming, leaving behind a void that echoed with silence. At first, I waited expectantly, hoping to hear from them soon. The days turned into weeks, and weeks into months, but the anticipated visits never resumed. The once vibrant connection faded into a distant memory.

The sudden cessation of these visits brought about a profound sense of loss. It was as if a chapter of companionship and shared moments had been abruptly closed. The routine returned, and the nursing home resumed its familiar, yet somewhat lonelier, atmosphere.

In the midst of this change, I found solace in the memories of the fleeting friendships. Although the visits ceased, the moments we shared remain etched in my mind. The transient nature of these connections taught me to appreciate the beauty of fleeting companionship and the importance of cherishing the moments, however brief.

Living in a nursing home has its challenges, but the ephemerality of these connections serves as a poignant reminder to value the present, embrace the unexpected, and find joy in the simplest moments, even if they are just passing through the corridors of our lives.

Epilogue

It's the little things that change first. At first, she would still come out with me, her steps slow but determined, her hand light on my arm as we made our way to the garden. Now, even those small ventures are too much. She rarely leaves her room these days, confined not by the walls of this nursing home, but by the frailty of a body that once carried her through a lifetime of love and labour.

I step into her room each morning, the light filtering in through thin curtains, casting soft patterns on the walls. She's usually sitting by the window, her walker within arm's reach, though she doesn't use it much anymore. She'll greet me with a smile, and I'll sit beside her, describing the world beyond her window. The jacarandas are in bloom, I'll say, their blossoms carpeting the ground like a purple quilt. She nods, her eyes bright with the memory of those walks we once took.

"I'll go for us," I tell her, and she always gives me that same small, knowing smile.

So I walk the short paths around the nursing home, past the flower beds and the old gum tree, letting the spring air fill my lungs. I stop at the bench and sit for a while, watching the world move on in its quiet, unhurried way. The magpies call, Bruce the kangaroo hops by, Fred the cockatoo cheers me on, children's voices drift faintly from a nearby school, and I think about how we used to laugh at the magpies' boldness, her teasing me about how they always seemed to target me during the nesting season.

When I return, she'll ask me about the garden, about the birds. I'll tell her everything, painting pictures with words, trying to bring a piece of the outside world into her small room. Even though she can't walk far now, we're still together in those moments, sharing the journey in our own way.

Made in United States
Cleveland, OH
20 June 2025

17862838R00089